Organizational Physics

The Science of Growing a Business

Lex Sisney

Santa Barbara, CA

Lex Sisney

Organizational Physics – The Science of Growing a Business

ISBN 978-1-300-78563-7

OrganizationalPhysics.com

Cover art by Seth Epstein

Edited by Elaine Johnson

"One of the best business books I have ever read, hands down. Steven Blank's *Four Steps to the Epiphany* meets Drucker's *Management* meets Tony Hsieh's *Happiness*. Sisney brings it all together into a practical framework being put into practice today by hundreds of entrepreneurs and executives worldwide.

If you're starting a business, Organizational Physics breaks down fundamental principles in market validation that cut time to revenue and ensures you are reaching the right market with the right products at the right time.

If you're trying to take your business to the next level, Organizational Physics will help you avoid the common mistakes businesses make in scaling and give you a toolset for growth.

If you're trying to reorganize your company and make sure you have the best people in the optimal positions with the proper management structures, Organizational Physics will help you create order out of chaos.

If you're trying to find that spark that made you first excited about your business or company, Organizational Physics will help you get it back and figure out how to sustain that exuberance and satisfaction necessary to inspire, lead, and be truly happy.

Most importantly, this is not an academic book. It is written from the perspective of a true innovator with a proven track record who has helped hundreds of companies and executives create successful businesses and achieve happiness and fulfillment along the way. You can read a lot of other books to gain guidance in niche areas of business, but few bring the principles together into a simple, powerful framework that can be put to use everyday in life and business.

Do yourself a favor and read this book. Don't tell your competition about it, though!"

- **Justin Bellante, CEO, BioIQ**

"In Organizational Physics, Lex Sisney has quietly produced a work of genius that should, in this reviewer's opinion, become the next major, and definitive, tome on business growth. It's comprehensive, exhaustive, and elegant. Lex spares no detail, offering the reader a totalizing framework for managing – and adeptly advancing through – every stage of an organization's lifespan, with the ultimate goal of perpetual growth and renewal. This is not merely a synthesis of great management and business growth theories; it is an original, and practical, blueprint for entrepreneurs, managers, and executives looking to scale their companies and lead fulfilling personal lives, all born out of the author's own hard-won business victories.

The book's fundamental distinction of energy, or integration, versus entropy is worth the cost of entry alone. It'll change both how you look at your long-range vision and how you approach short-term, day-to-day task management. But that's just the foundation for what becomes a staggering number of insights – the Four Styles of Management; the Seven Stages of the Execution Lifecycle; the Three Strategic Follies; the Pre-Startup Checklist; and countless other 'gems' and epiphanies – all interwoven into an actionable, dynamic system uniquely suited for a world characterized by endless change, chaos, and disruption.

In short, if you're starting, managing, or scaling an organization and don't read Organizational Physics, you'll be missing out on one of the most important developments in modern business theory and practice. If you do, you may just find the clearest path to the glory, victory, and riches – in all the senses of that word – inherent in the promise of the entrepreneurial dream."

- **Sam Rosen, CEO, ThoughtLead**

"As a founder of a tech information security company, I found this book to be incredibly useful. All the examples and anecdotes described in this book represent so many of the lessons I learned the hard way (and wish I learned the easy way) that I recommend this for any startup team. If you are like me, a founder who built and grew an organization using a tech foundation background, you'll find the characteristics of the personality types described in a way such that you'll really grok it. We have since leveraged the Organizational Physics new hire assessments to add an additional element to our hiring process. The book's metaphor for various organizational and psychological components of your organization leverages the laws of physics which tech entrepreneurs should really be able to relate to; any entrepreneur should be able to see how entropy impacts their organization. Personally, I found Lex's description of working in your 'genius zone' to be a really helpful way to view and orient my role in a way that maximizes my satisfaction and effectiveness. Definitely required reading."

- **John Abraham, Founder and CTO, Redspin, Inc.**

"In the midst of our pursuits, we too often fail to step back and ask obvious but important questions. What really am I trying to accomplish? How do I define success? Where am I expending energy and not seeing a return? Organizational Physics helps answer those questions by providing a framework for breaking down your business (and life) to its functional core. In a wonderful marriage of Eastern and Western philosophies, science and art, Lex's revelatory approach allows you to assess your circumstances and take decisive action. It is impossible not to reap massive rewards from spending time with Lex – and, having worked with him, I can say without fear of overstatement that humanity would benefit if everyone followed the principles he puts forth."

 - **Ophir Tanz, CEO, GumGum**

"There are plenty of books that articulate the tactics of growing or stabilizing a business. Most try to sell you a specific technique. While tactics and strategies are clearly discussed, you'll find that Organizational Physics digs much deeper into the core of what makes a business tick. This is an all out deconstruction at an atomic level of what drives the success and failure of companies. What starts as a metaphor for business, chapter by chapter, slowly becomes an enlightened journey describing the flow of energy in relation to your business. Through this deeper understanding you begin to recognize the patterns and relationships that lend themselves to profit or loss.

Everything we perceive is predicated on the fundamental laws of the Universe. As Organizational Physics unfolds, you realize your business responds to these same forces and principals. Turn your attention to the underlying principles. Things that are universally true and that transcend any particular company or situation will always be true. If you want to succeed in business, or in life, quit trying to replace principles with techniques. Instead, read this book, apply the principles and thrive."

 - **Matt Cooper, CEO, Addroid**

"Organizational Physics is both enjoyable and inspirational. And unlike most modern business books filled with trendy lessons, this book provides a durable framework that can adapt to all types of situations.

While this book is perfect for CEOs and other high-level execs, you don't need to be part of a fast-scaling organization to learn from this book. You can apply its lessons about the destructive power of entropy to all types of lessons in your daily life, not just your career.

I highly recommend this book."

   - **Darren Litt, CEO, GoLive! Mobile**

"Lex Sisney has nailed it with Organizational Physics. The concepts provide an amazing framework for making decisions, assessing your environment, and taking action. The whole idea of how to get energy and neutralize or eliminate entropy in your life is totally liberating. The stuff that brings you down: eliminate it. The book has also helped me find my Genius Zone – that place where I operate as well as anyone else in the world, where I feel light, confident, and capable. Staying in your Genius Zone is your goal. Get there. Maybe the most valuable insights for me are how I not only assess myself with Lex's PSIU framework but how I have become more aware of other's styles. By understanding the people around me I am better able to make progress with many different types of personalities. I'm also able to be smart about how I build a team, acknowledging that complementary styles are a winning combination. If you are an entrepreneur or aspire to be one, give Organizational Physics a read. You'll be glad you did."

   - **Russell Benaroya, CEO, EveryMove**

"We're all getting advice, even if we don't know it. The advice comes in many forms. From gurus, experts, society, the media, our parents – everywhere. Usually, this advice is counterproductive and makes a tough situation even tougher to figure out. What I like best about Organizational Physics is that it provides the framework to answer life's most perplexing issues, not by going outside yourself, but by relying on your own inner guidance.

The other thing I appreciate about this book is that it really calls out the interdependence between our lives as individuals and how we operate within a larger system. This gave me a heightened awareness as to what matters most. If the tools outlined in Organizational Physics aren't working for you, chances are you aren't being honest with yourself. Or perhaps you are ignoring the indicators the system is providing. If you're operating in unchartered territory, read this book and apply its principles and you'll know what to do next."

   - **Seth Zaharako, CEO, Overthinking**

Contents

Acknowledgements

The purpose of this book is to equip entrepreneurs, CEOs, and team leaders with a complete system for successfully growing their organizations and have more satisfaction doing it. My approach is unique in bringing together two formerly distinct and separate disciplines: organizational performance and the physical sciences. While organizational development has usually been viewed as "soft" discipline and the physical sciences as "hard" disciplines, there is powerful insight that can be found in the common ground between them. Without the astonishing, breakthrough work of thought leaders from both disciplines, this book would not have been possible.

Within the realm of organizational theory, the work of Dr. Ichak Adizes has made a profound impact in my understanding of corporate lifecycles, management styles, decision making, and the inherent conflict between efficiency and effectiveness.

Geoffrey Moore of the Chasm Group in San Bruno, California, has helped me understand the nuances of selling to certain customer types at distinct stages of the product/market lifecycle. Thought leaders like Steve Blank and Eric Reis, as well as the principles of agile software development, have helped me to recognize that there's a process to follow to navigate the product/market lifecycle.

I am grateful to Seth Godin, Guy Kawasaki, and Howard Bloom for continually reminding me what I've always known in my heart—that business is ultimately about passion and contribution to others.

When it comes to the physical sciences, this book will reference the luminaries of classical physics, as well as biology and systems theory. These include Ludwig von Bertalanffy, one of the founders of general systems theory, who helped us see that systems are everywhere and exhibit some common properties; Edward Lorenz, the mathematician and meteorologist who worked in obscurity while identifying the principles of chaos theory; Charles Darwin, the legendary biologist and grandfather of evolutionary theory who recognized that the single greatest mistake a species can make is to fail to adapt to its environment; Rudolf Clausius, who introduced the world to the principles of thermodynamics and the concept of entropy; and, of course, the greatest classical physicist, Isaac Newton, who helped us understand the laws of motion and momentum.

While the formal knowledge I've gleaned from these luminaries is immense, equally priceless are the lessons learned from my peers in the trenches of entrepreneurship. These include my partners and staff in the businesses I've run, my clients, and colleagues with whom I've had the privilege of collaborating. In particular, I would like to acknowledge Sunil Dovedy, Seth Epstein, Kelly Foy, John Greathouse, Per Pettersen, Sam Rosen, and Ian Silverberg.

A special thank you goes to my editor Elaine Johnson for her excellent work under tight deadlines and in the eleventh hour.

Most importantly, I am grateful to my amazing and talented wife Linda Nurra for her love, support, wisdom, and insightful feedback throughout the writing process and beyond. I am a very lucky man.

Introduction

I f you're a growth-oriented CEO, entrepreneur, or department manager, then you're naturally under pressure to lead your business to greater levels of performance. You also need to do this in a fast-moving, turbulent, evolving marketplace. A lot is riding on your leadership and there's little room for error. There's time pressure, money pressure, market pressure—not to mention work/life balance pressure—that can all add to the difficulty of achieving success.

Complicating matters is that there never seems to be enough time and energy to accomplish everything that needs to get done. Using limited resources, you must drive success, build powerhouse teams, set the right priorities, and execute fast. And because the right plan is only as good as your team's commitment to implementing it, you have to ensure constant buy-in and continually lower the friction that gets in the way.

That's a tall order. If you're honest with yourself, you'll admit there are countless times when you're feeling stressed, doubtful, unclear, or simply stuck. Sometimes your job can feel so thrilling, you can't imagine doing anything else. Other times it feels so frustrating that you want to quit, move to Tahiti, and take up painting. All in all, you've chosen a career path filled with adventure, danger, excitement, and the opportunity to manage one mini-crisis after another.

As a wise leader, you have learned to trust in your own experience. But you also keep an eye and ear open for valuable insights and perspectives. In this regard, there are countless management theories and organizational practices that you can choose from. There are top-down, bottom-up, agile-iterative, data-driven, design-first, customer-oriented, outcome-based, decentralized, centralized, democratic, autocratic, process-driven, lifecycle-stages, and X-Y-Z management theories. If you ask a dozen entrepreneurs, CEOs, and management experts which is the best model, you'll hear as many different answers.

When you're faced with a myriad of challenges, opportunities, constraints, and choices, how can you decisively lead your organization where you want it to go? When can you trust your past experience and when does it cast blinders on your ability to see clearly? What's the right approach for your particular situation? How do you maximize your organization's performance and your personal satisfaction, now and in the future?

The answer, as with all things, is to first understand what's really going on. For example, a good doctor understands how the body really functions. Rather than focusing on symptoms, s/he will work to understand the systemic causes of a disease. Similarly, if you understand how your business and team really work beneath the surface, you can get at the underlying causes of what's making them fail or succeed.

The purpose of this book is to do just that—to explain how your business really works and to provide you with a complete system for improving its performance. What I'm proposing is a universal, meta-level approach to solving any business problem or condition. You can use it to support your company's overall success, boost the effectiveness of your teams, select and implement your chosen strategy, and even help yourself and others maximize their job satisfaction. It's an all-encompassing approach to individual and organizational transformation.

But how is it that, without ever having met you, studied your business, or probably even worked in your industry (not to mention the fact that every business is unique), I could possibly tell you how your business really works and how to improve it? The reason is that I'm not relying on any context-specific business theory—but rather synthesizing certain principles of general management theory with a totally different discipline: the field of physics.

Physics is the study of matter and energy and their interactions. Its aim is to understand how nature at its most basic level really works. You can say that physics is the most fundamental of all sciences because physical laws can explain many observable facts in biology, medicine, chemistry, engineering, and other disciplines. It is so pervasive in its applications that it also applies to *your* situation, regardless of how unique it may seem.

At its core, physics provides us with a universal lens, language, and sequence to follow to understand nature's underlying properties, patterns, and behaviors. For example, Einstein's famous physics equation $E=MC^2$ provides a lens, or a way of looking at the world, that is both elegant and enlightening. It also provides a language that translates beyond geographies, cultures, and culture-bound languages. A physicist in Beijing and one in Paris can communicate effectively using only the language of their discipline. Finally, physics provides a sequence to follow. If you repeat certain conditions in this way, then this will be your result, regardless of the time or place.

All systems—whether electrical, biological, or social—have common patterns, behaviors, and properties that can be understood and give us greater insight into their behavior. What if it were possible to apply the laws of physics to better understand the performance of your organization? Not only would we reveal the underlying patterns driving organizational performance, but we would also have a common lens, language, and sequence to use to improve that performance.

The premise of this book is that it is both possible and extremely productive to do just that. There are indeed some basic laws of nature that determine the performance of any organization. Put another way, certain classic laws of physics apply not only to physical systems such as stars, toasters, and spaceships, but also to complex adaptive systems such as individuals, families, companies, and countries. In a word, we call these complex adaptive systems "organizations." If physics is the science of matter and energy and their interactions, and "management" refers to principles and methods used to lead organizations, then Organizational Physics is the translation, or the common ground, between the two.

In my work with high-tech companies, CEOs, entrepreneurs, and organizational leaders, I have found that this translation is not only interesting—it's essential. Technological advance continues unremittingly, yet most of our existing management paradigms are lagging behind the times. To many, it seems that the world is at a dangerous tipping point—that we keep running faster and faster without a compass while heading in the wrong direction. Without a management system that takes this into account, organizations will have a harder time orchestrating positive outcomes. We'll be stuck in the tower of Babel of conflicting management theories that just don't decode quickly enough for our new era. This book argues that the models of physics offer answers to the question of how to keep up—in ways that are powerful, practical, sustainable, and universally valid.

~~~

There are **Six Laws of Organizational Physics**. These laws determine an organization's performance and can help you improve it. They can be found within core branches of physics, including systems theory, thermodynamics, and motion, as well as the most fundamental principle of evolution: adaptation. Think of it this way: If you want your organization to thrive rather than fail, move swiftly in a chosen direction, adapt successfully to change, and behave in a certain way, then the answers all reside within these laws.

Below is a brief explanation of each law and why—as an entrepreneur, manager, or leader—you should understand its implications.

1. An organization is a complex adaptive system.

Organizations are *complex* in that they have many interconnected and interdependent elements, subsystems, or parts. They are *adaptive* in that they shape and respond to changes in the surrounding environment. They are *systems* in that they respond as a whole organization, not just as a collection of parts. To understand how something really works, it's not enough to break it down into its components. You must look at it in the context of the complete system. Viewing an organization as a complex adaptive system provides valuable insights into how it functions *in its totality*.

2. **An organization is subject to the first law of thermodynamics.**

   The first law of thermodynamics states that, at any given point in time, a system has a finite amount of energy. If an organization is to get new energy, it must get it from its environment. For a business, energy is any usable source of power such as money, resources, and market clout. Its environment includes the surrounding system of customers, social norms, regulations, and economies in which it operates. If there's high integration between an organization's capabilities and the opportunities in the environment, then the organization can receive an abundance of new energy and be successful. If there's no integration between them, then there's no new energy created for the organization and—like a man on a desert island without food and water—it will soon perish.

3. **An organization is subject to the second law of thermodynamics.**

   The second law of thermodynamics indicates that everything falls apart over time. This is due to entropy, which is disorder or disintegration. All systems are subject to it; none can escape it. An organization's available energy first flows to manage and counter the disintegrating force of entropy. If entropy in the system is high, then it costs the system a higher amount of its available energy to maintain itself and get work done. Therefore, it has less energy available to drive integration forward in its environment. To get an immediate, intuitive grasp of this principle, just imagine a business with a great market opportunity but which also suffers from high internal friction, politicking, and infighting. It takes a tremendous amount of energy to get any work done and the business can't capture the external opportunity as a result. How an organization manages its available energy is what ultimately determines its failure or success.

4. **An organization must shape and respond to its environment and do so as a whole system, including its parts and sub-parts.**

   In physics, a chaotic system is one that seems random in its behavior but is actually driven by some basic repeating patterns or forces that exist from the macro- to the micro-level. In this regard, an organization is like a chaotic system. It has patterns or forces that exist all throughout the organization, from the smallest tasks and behaviors to the largest enterprise. These forces can be mapped in many ways. One of the most effective I know is placing them along two basic parameters or axes: (1) how the organization *shapes* and *responds to* its environment; and (2) how the organization manages its individual parts and the whole.

Later you will learn how these parameters explain four primary forces within an organization and how these give rise to individual and collective behavior. They are called the Producing, Stabilizing, Innovating, and Unifying forces. Each of these expresses itself through a particular behavior pattern. If one or more of the forces are absent, the organization will perish. Understanding them allows you to work at the root causes of what's happening in the system and use them to create desired change.

5. **An organization is subject to the conditions of its environment.**

The driving principle of evolution shows that it is not the strongest or most intelligent that survive but those that are best adapted to their environment. Therefore, the greatest mistake an organization can make is to misread its environment. If it does, it will cease to get new energy and it will fail. Because the environment is always changing, the organization must always be adapting. Successful adaptation requires a constant realignment among the organization's capabilities to execute (Execution Lifecycle), its markets or customers (Market Lifecycle), and its products (Product Lifecycle). How an organization manages this alignment is *the basis of its strategy.*

6. **An organization is subject to the laws of motion.**

Newton's three laws of motion reveal the principles of movement for physical objects in the universe. The laws explain inertia, acceleration, and reaction. The laws also help us understand and work with the principles of organizational change and momentum. Namely, they explain why an organization will tend to behave the way it does unless a force of change causes it to do something differently. They explain how the mass of an organization naturally resists change and how every action performed in the business creates an equal and opposite reaction that must be managed. How an organization manages its mass determines *the speed of its execution.*

This is just a brief summary of the six laws that govern organizational performance. Don't worry if they don't make too much sense yet. They'll become crystal clear as you read the rest of this book. As you deepen your understanding of each law, you'll be able to spot it everywhere around you—in your family, your social circle, your community, your government, and beyond. In other words, you'll find that these meta-laws hold true regardless of the time, place, or type of organization. Too often, management theory presupposes that work and life are separate things. They're not! Soon you'll become skilled at quickly spotting the principles everywhere—and when you can do that, you'll be able to see them at work in your business too.

You'll also find that, in this process, you're becoming a more astute and powerful leader. You can now be placed in any situation and instantly understand what caused it to get that way, as well as predict and prevent future problems. You'll have deeper insight into why people and teams show up the way they do. Finally, you'll better understand certain principles of strategy, finance, and product development to bring the entire organization together to execute fast and well.

I'd like to share a caveat about using physics as a management methodology. I've tried to align the laws of Organizational Physics as closely as possible to the laws of classic physics, but there are differences in interpretations. This is natural. Physics studies the nuts and bolts of the physical world—and human organizations are much more than that. At the back of this book, you'll find an appendix where I explain some differences and show why the laws of Organizational Physics are nevertheless both physics-based and applicable to human organizations.

There's an old joke about two physicists in a classroom. They're at the chalkboard, on which one of them has written a complicated formula in three steps. Step 1 is a proven known. Step 3 is also a proven known. In between them, Step 2 reads: "Then a miracle occurs." His partner looks at the board and says, "I think you need to be more specific here in Step 2."

So let's not forget that countless unknowns exist and that any framework, even one as authoritative as physics, is just that—a framework. Your own drive, skills, experience, capabilities, resources, and support systems are what make any theory come alive.

Finally, I'd like to say a few things about the audience for whom this book was written. Although the laws of Organizational Physics apply to most situations and organizations of all sizes, this book was created for leaders, entrepreneurs, and managers working with *start-up to expansion-stage technology-based companies*. This is so for three reasons:

> 1) My own background is in building expansion-stage technology businesses. I've done this successfully as an entrepreneur and as a coach to other successful entrepreneurs and management teams. This is an audience that I know well and I can speak firsthand to their challenges and opportunities. My work as a coach and

consultant motivates me to share my methods with all those who can benefit and expand the reach and impact of Organizational Physics around the world.

2) The speed and disruptive change of technology-based markets make this industry willing to try on new methods and require it to produce results quickly. This is a perfect proving ground filled with bright, passionate early adopters who appreciate cutting-edge thought leadership. It is this sector that drives forward innovations that are later adopted by other industries.

3) The world is now struggling with complexity in profound ways. It's not just "too much information" and noise, but an inability to integrate all the data in a cohesive way and to make wise decisions based on it. It's becoming clear to many that government won't save us, but rather a cadre of agile, innovative organizations woven together by a passion for technology, ecology, and creating better ways of living and working. I am passionate about building World 2.0 with this group.

That said, even if you're not involved with a high-tech company, you will still gain powerful insights into how your organization functions, as well as clarity on the concrete steps you can take to be a better manager and leader. Just read it with a filter on and apply the lessons to your own organization.

Striving to find the underlying principles that govern how something performs is not a new quest. It's been around since before humans looked at fire and thought, "How does it work?" And ever since the advent of the scientific method and the printing press, our shared comprehension of how things actually work continues to increase at a staggering rate. As our collective knowledge grows, we continue to ask, "How does it really work?" and new discoveries are made.

So with that spirit of discovery in mind, I invite you to think of the organization you'd most like to improve and ask yourself, "Hmmm, I wonder, how it really works?" Then dive into the world of Organizational Physics for the answers.

How to Read This Book

In Dan Brown's bestselling novel, *The Da Vinci Code*, the protagonist discovers a coded treasure map. He intuitively knows that the map is valuable, but it's impossible to decipher it without knowing the code. In fact, to an untrained eye, the map looks like gibberish.

While similarly cryptic at first, the map of Organizational Physics provides those who understand it with priceless value. In this case, the map unlocks the code to understanding why an organization behaves the way it does and how you can improve its performance. But don't worry—I won't take you through a suspense novel plot to get the answers. I'm going to give you the basics right now. Rather than try to interpret too much too soon, however, just familiarize yourself with the layout and prime your brain for what's ahead.

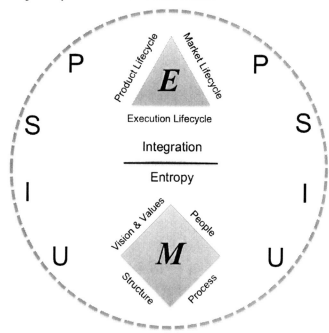

Figure 1. The Organizational Physics Map.

This book is divided into four parts, each of which focuses on a key section of the Organizational Physics map. I suggest you first read the parts in order because each one builds on the previous. Once you're familiar with the overall concepts, use the book as a field guide for when a particular issue or situation arises. For example, if you think you might be headed into a Strategic Folly, turn to Part III, or if you want a refresher on how to best manage an Innovator, turn to Part II, and so on.

O Captain! My Captain!

Here's a metaphor to aid your immediate and intuitive understanding of the Organizational Physics map. Imagine that you're the captain of a sailboat about to embark on a long-distance race at sea. Your goal is to lead your crew, set your course, optimize performance, and win the race. This map shows you how.

The dotted circle is the entire organization—the boat, sail, crew, etc. It's drawn as a circle because the organization isn't just a collection of parts; it's a whole system that can be as large or as small as you define it. It's dotted because there isn't a solid boundary—elements of the organization interact with both each other and the external environment or market, just as the boat interacts with the wind and sea.

At the top of the map is the *Strategy Pyramid*. This is the sail that powers the boat by getting new energy (E) from the environment. Without new energy, the boat isn't going to go anywhere. In order to get new energy, the sail must constantly be adjusted to catch the wind, just as a business must constantly align the products it sells with the markets it serves, and with its capabilities to execute. Markets, products, and capabilities—just like the currents, tides, and seasons—exist in a pattern or lifecycle. When you can learn to spot the pattern, you can sail much faster than a captain who can't.

At the bottom of the map is the *Execution Diamond*. It represents the mass (M) of the boat, equipment, and crew. The mass of the boat has inertia and every action on the boat has an equal and opposite reaction. In order for the boat to sail fast, you need to get its collective mass headed in the right direction while simultaneously adapting to changing seas and conditions. You do this by aligning the Vision and Values, Structure, Processes, and People around your goal.

"PSIU" at the edges of the map stands for the *Producing, Stabilizing, Innovating,* and *Unifying* forces. The forces show up as innate characteristics of you, your crew, and the work that needs to be performed throughout the journey. These forces show us how all aspects of the system, from the micro to the macro, shape and respond to the environment in different ways.

In the center of the map are the words "Integration/Entropy." "Integration" indicates the amount of new energy made available to the ship from the environment. "Entropy" indicates the amount of available energy spent maintaining the ship and crew, making decisions, and getting the work done. Together they reveal how available energy is allocated within the organization and ultimately determine if you can sail fast and win the race. If too much energy is lost in managing against the onslaught of entropy, the boat will sail slowly and ultimately sink.

Every captain must prepare to win the race. Being a good captain, you first assess the overall environment. What are the prevailing winds? How are the currents flowing? What is the best route to win the race? Critically, what type of a captain are you? Are you a Producer who prefers to focus on a short-term goal and drive hard? Are you a Stabilizer who prefers to plan, structure, and organize for an efficient journey and make contingency plans? Are you an Innovator who senses the storms and opportunities on the horizon and comes up with creative new inventions for superior performance? Are you a Unifier who values good teamwork and camaraderie? Or are you some combination of these? Whatever the answer, it's vital to recognize that no captain can go it alone. You need to surround yourself with a complementary crew. It takes an entire ship to achieve great performance.

Second, look at the mass of the boat and crew. How is it behaving? Is it producing results? Is it so stable, heavy, and bureaucratic that it can't respond to changes in the wind and sea? Is it able to adapt to changes and innovate with new solutions to vexing problems? Is the crew unified and acting as one? You'll also need to make sure that the key subsystems of the boat are in alignment. Do you have aligned *Vision and Values*? Is the *Structure* of the boat right for this race? Do you have a *Process* in place to ensure that good racing decisions are made and implemented quickly? Finally, does the crew have the right mix of *People* to create a high-performing team?

Third, you chart your course. This means that you must get energy from the environment by aligning your strategy so that the wind is in your sails. To get the wind in your sails and produce new energy (E) in the form of money, resources, and clout, you must align the *Product* (the assets you make available for sale), *Market* (the types of customers you're targeting), and *Execution* (the organization's ability to execute) *lifecycles*. If you have good alignment, you will have good timing relative to the wind and sea conditions. But good alignment also takes constant readjustment. As the captain, you must make sure that the crew is producing results. You must provide the right level of stabilization so that everything is organized and systematized but also flexible and responsive. You must keep your eye on the horizon and innovate to changing conditions. And you must make sure that the entire system is unified and acts in concert.

When you're out at sea, you must make sure that the boat is well integrated with the surrounding conditions so that the energy produced by the wind in the sails is greater than the mass of the boat and crew. That's the secret to fast speeds. However, a good captain can't just focus on the external sea. He also has to pay attention to the internal workings of the ship. Entropy is always attacking a boat at sea, just as it attacks every other organization. Things eat away at it from the inside. If the internal energy and resource needs of the ship are too high (think of a crack in the hull, a torn sail, a misaligned tiller, or a mutiny by the crew), then the ship will lose its effectiveness and stall. If it flounders at sea for too long, all hands will be lost.

Being an entrepreneur is equally—if not more—challenging. Countless unknowns exist, the market changes, storms arise, and the competition improves. But you already know all this. In fact, you welcome the challenge. It can be an incredibly thrilling ride filled with loot, camaraderie, and epic adventure.

When you're out racing, keep in mind that there are basically two types of captains, just as there are two types of entrepreneurs: one wise and the other foolish. The foolish captain attempts to predict the seas, currents, and seasonal storms; plot the right course; and make a dash for the finish line. This is foolish because there are just too many things outside of the captain's control. Similarly, foolish entrepreneurs attempt to time the market, quickly attract users, and sell the company off at just the right time. One bad storm will quickly destroy an ill-prepared organization. The wise captain or entrepreneur, recognizing that the sea is always changing and impossible to predict, focuses on building a sea-worthy, sustainable ship from top to bottom.

There's an old proverb that says, "You can't control the wind and tides but you can adjust your sails." That's the goal of this book: to equip you with the knowledge to run a fast, sea-worthy ship with a great crew and to adjust your sails at the right time to win the race.

Now let's get started!

Lex Sisney

Part I - Drive Sustainable Success and Satisfaction

Lex Sisney

1. The Universal Success Formula

What makes something fail or succeed? As I write this, there are 126,936 books on Amazon.com that try to answer this question. If you were to peruse them, you'd find various answers on how to be more successful. "Work hard." "Be persistent." "Set your goals." "Change your thinking, change your life." "Influence and network with others." "Find the right opportunity." "Invest in your future." "Eat less. Exercise more." "It's not what you know but who you know." The list goes on. While the authors of these books have valuable perspectives to offer, very few of them have tried to answer the *deepest* level of the question "why does something fail or succeed?"

What makes something fail or succeed is truly a deep and universal question. If there were a universal answer, you could use it to focus your efforts on what makes the biggest difference in your success. It would shed considerable light on past events and offer a framework to follow going forward.

The surprising thing is that, beyond getting the "details" and "circumstances" right, there is ultimately one determinant of failure or success. This is true for businesses as it is for individuals, families, schools, communities, governments, and even your favorite NFL team. It also applies to any definition of success you can think of: earn a billion dollars, attain enlightenment, feel happy, get laid, be fit and healthy, live the four-hour work week, or whatever.

Take that in for a moment. One thing—and one thing only—ultimately determines the success of everything. That includes the success of everything that exists now, that has ever existed, or that will ever exist. If you knew what this one thing was, you'd not only be able to improve your own chances of success, but you could also tell whether other things around you will fail or succeed. Is this company a good investment? Will this couple make a happy partnership? Will my team win the championship? You'd know the answers with much greater clarity.

What you're about to learn is very powerful stuff. It seems simple at first—so simple that many people miss its significance. And while some classic laws of physics explain it, you don't need a degree in physics to understand it. In fact, the one thing that determines failure or success is so blindly obvious that once you understand it, you'll notice its effects everywhere you look.

The Secret to Sustainable Success

If you want to understand how something really works and what makes it successful, it's not enough to break it down into its individual components. Instead, you need to look at how it operates as a *system*. By definition, a system is *a series of interacting, interrelated, or interdependent elements forming a complex whole.* And there's absolutely nothing you can think of that is not a system.

For example, you're a system (specifically, a complex adaptive or living system). You have a body, which is a physical system comprised of other systems (immune, circulatory, digestive, etc.). If we were to look closely at any one of these, we'd see that they're comprised of even smaller systems. And of course, your physical system is also an element within larger systems that include your mind, emotions, family, community, economy, government, planet, and so on. Everything is a system.

When it comes to the study of what makes something successful, what we're really asking is what causes a complex adaptive system to fail or succeed. Success simply means that the system (e.g., you, your family, your company, or whatever you choose to identify as the system) attains a desired goal. Failure means it does not. Winning the Super Bowl . . . being happy . . . earning a billion dollars—as long as you can measure it quantitatively or qualitatively, it's a valid definition of success. And because everything, large or small, is a system, we can use the same universal principles to understand if it's likely to fail or succeed. That's pretty cool.

What actually does cause any system to fail or succeed? The answer is *System Energy Management.* This means just what it sounds like: System Energy Management refers to how energy behaves within a system.

Two laws of physics dictate how energy is used within a system. They're called the first and second law of thermodynamics. Engineers use the laws of thermodynamics to design everything from buildings and bridges to microchips and spaceships. We can also use these same laws to understand how energy behaves within an organization.

The first law of thermodynamics is called "conservation." It tells us that, at any given point in time, the potential energy available to a system is finite. Whether we're referring to your family or your business, this has a finite amount of potential energy available to it. In order to get new energy, the system must acquire it from the surrounding environment—just like you must get food from the refrigerator or your business must get sales from its customers.

The second law of thermodynamics is called "entropy." It tells us that every system falls apart over time. No matter how hard we try, there's no escaping the irresistible force of entropy. In *The Nature of the Physical World*, Sir Arthur Eddington aptly put it this way:

> The law that entropy always increases holds … the supreme position among the laws of Nature. If someone points out to you that your pet theory of the universe is in disagreement with Maxwell's equations—then so much the worse for Maxwell's equations. … But if your theory is found to be against the second law of thermodynamics I can give you no hope; there is nothing for it but to collapse in deepest humiliation.[1]

You, me, and everything in the universe are ultimately falling apart over time. Wherever we find aging, disintegration, deterioration, and disorder we're looking at entropy at work.

To understand how the laws of thermodynamics fit into organizational theory, then, just remember that every system has a finite amount of potential energy and every system is falling apart over time. Simple. Now that you know these two laws, you can begin to use them to understand if your organization or any other system in the universe is likely to fail or succeed. You do that by understanding the universal success formula:[2]

$$\text{Success} = \Sigma \left[\frac{\text{Integration}}{\text{Entropy}} \right]$$

Figure 2. The Universal Success Formula.

The universal success formula shows that success is just a function of two things: integration over entropy. Let's define the terms and then explain how this works. As you already know, success is any goal you desire to attain: making a lot of money, falling in love, being fit and

---

[1] Sir Author Eddington, *The Nature of the Physical World* (London: J.M. Dent & Sons, 1935).

[2] The Universal Success Formula is a development of the success formula created by Dr. Ichak Adizes of the Adizes Institute. Adizes argued that success is a function of "External Marketing" over "Internal Marketing." See Ichak Adizes, *Mastering Change: The Power of Mutual Trust and Respect* (Santa Barbara: The Adizes Institute Publishing, 1991) and *Managing Corporate Lifecycles* (Upper Saddle River, NJ: Prentice Hall, 1999).

healthy, raising a family, or growing your business. It doesn't matter how you define it.

Integration is a measure of how much energy the system is getting from its environment. Energy in this case is anything useful and desirable that can be made productive in the pursuit of success (money, resources, clout, etc.). High integration is good. Low integration is bad. Why? Because when there's high integration between a system and its environment, the system has aligned its capabilities with opportunities and can extract available energy. It can use this energy to grow and be successful. If there's no integration, then there's no new energy available to the system and it will fail. I will explain the elements of integration and how to increase it more fully in Part III: How to Choose the Right Strategy.

$$\text{Success} = \Sigma \left[\frac{\text{Integration}}{\text{Entropy}} \right]$$

Available energy first flows here

Figure 3. Available energy first flows to manage entropy needs.

Entropy in the formula indicates the amount of energy required to maintain the system, make decisions, and get work done. Low entropy is good. High entropy is bad. Why? We know from the first law of thermodynamics that, at any given point in time, the potential amount of energy available to a system is finite. We also know from the second law of thermodynamics that the force of entropy is constantly eating away at a system. And here's where it gets profound: The energy available to a system must always flow first to manage its entropy needs. Only after those needs are met, and if any energy is left over, will it be made available for integration. Therefore, the higher the level of entropy, the lower the level of potential success. And if entropy gets too high, the system will fail and perish.

How Entropy Shows Up in a System

The fact that available energy first flows to manage a system's internal entropy needs is a universal law. It applies to all systems, big or small. Let's take a look at some everyday examples to see how prevalent this law is in your everyday experience.

Imagine you go to visit a friend in the hospital who is recovering from cancer. Cancer—or any physical ailment—is really an entropy problem. Your friend is a system with a fixed amount of available energy. The energy use must first flow within the system so it can maintain itself. Because your friend is sick, he needs most of his available energy to heal. When you visit your friend at the hospital, the doctors will ask you to limit your visitation time. They intuitively recognize that your friend needs to conserve as much energy as possible to heal. He has very little left over to engage in conversation (integration) with you.

Sports is a great landscape to view the dynamic between integration and entropy. Let's take the example of Randy Moss, the National Football League (NFL) receiver. He's famous for his world-class capabilities (running fast, leaping high, and catching a football) and there's an opportunity to apply those capabilities in the NFL. However, Randy is also infamous for increasing entropy in the locker room. Coaches often call it shifting a locker room from "we-focused" to "me-focused." If you were a GM or a coach, you would weigh your desire to have Randy on your team based upon how you view the increase in team capability over a potential increase in team entropy. And be warned, if the entropy gets high enough, you're not going to be successful no matter how good the skills of your individual players are.

Next, imagine a family going through a divorce. The family system is succumbing to entropy so its members will have less energy available to be effective both within the family and out in the world. The kids are not as successful at school because the lack of harmony costs them more energy to manage their own mental and emotional states. The parents put on a smile at work but the divorce weighs heavily and thus lowers their productivity. The energy drains will continue until the family members make peace and accept the new reality (or, by some other means, recapture the energy now being lost to entropy).

If you've ever felt hurt, angry, or betrayed (and who hasn't?), then you know that these emotions leave you with less energy, zeal, and awareness to bring to your job. Yet another entropy problem! Your mental and emotional states are systems subject to the laws of thermodynamics. When your mind and emotions are draining your energy, the system needs more energy to maintain itself and there will be less energy available for you to be engaged and productive.

Picture a company with a growing opportunity in the marketplace and with unique capabilities to exploit it but whose co-founders are at each other's throats. There's mistrust and a lack of respect that impact how sales, marketing, finance, and technology plan, communicate, and work together. This is an entropy problem. It costs too much energy to maintain the system against this onslaught and the company won't be able to marshal its resources effectively to capture the opportunity. Unless the current energy drains can be freed up, the company will succumb to entropy and perish (specifically, the company loses its ability to integrate—i.e., make sales, meet customer needs, and adapt to changing conditions in the market—because the internal friction is too high).

As I write this, the U.S. economy is near 10 percent unemployment in most areas, the highest it's been since the great depression. Can the U.S. government craft policies to get people back to work in quality jobs? Clearly, the government has capabilities to legislate, tax, and use force. There are opportunities in the country for government to be of service: job programs, healthcare programs, defense programs, education programs, and the list goes on. At the same time, the political climate is rife with entropy. There's a lot of politicking, finger pointing, positioning for sound bites, right versus left, etc. There don't seem to be a lot of thoughtful, considerate, long-term policy decisions or a vision to improve integration of the country. Unless there's a decrease in entropy within the political system, or unless the entropy gets so great that the system collapses on itself, you can expect more of the same.

It's also revealing to look at global issues through the lens of integration and entropy. Climate change is an entropy problem. The science indicates that man-made carbon emissions are increasing and climate change is occurring. But if you are a climate change skeptic, you likely view economic integration as paramount and will argue that any increase in entropy within the biosphere (e.g., rising sea levels, ocean acidification, and loss of habitat) isn't caused by humans, can't be helped, or won't cause a serious impact. If, on the other hand, you recognize the reality of climate change, then you likely view limiting the entropy caused by carbon emissions as the world's top priority. You recognize that if the biosphere goes, all of humanity goes with it and that any economic integration should be in service to the whole system—not the other way around.

The Key to a Thriving Business

Now that you're familiar with some signs of entropy in everyday life, you'll be able to better understand its negative impact on your business. For example, imagine that your company has 100 arbitrary points of energy and that 50 of them are needed to maintain the system, make decisions, and get work done. This would leave 50 points available to do integration—in other words, to find opportunities, build your capabilities, make sales, and so on. In this case, be wary. Ignore entropy at your peril.

$$Success = \Sigma \left[\frac{50}{50} \right] \quad \boxed{Warning}$$

Figure 4. High entropy steals from high success.

Now imagine that you're able to decrease your internal energy needs by half, to 25 points. That leaves 75 points available for integration. This is a 300 percent improvement in your top-line performance. You now have that much more energy to integrate new opportunities, develop new capabilities, make sales, etc. This is awesome.

$$Success = \Sigma \left[\frac{75}{25} \right] \quad \boxed{Success!}$$

Figure 5. A decrease in entropy allows the system to have more energy for top-line performance.

One question I'm often asked about the application of the laws of thermodynamics to business is this: "Is my company's available energy really fixed? Can't I go out and raise more capital, get a new sale, or complete a merger or acquisition and thus increase my available energy?" The answer is yes, you can—and only as long as the amount of energy needed to keep entropy in check is less than the amount of new energy you can get from the environment. There's an old adage in business that says: "I've never seen a problem big enough that another sale can't solve!" This is true as long as integration is greater than entropy (i.e., revenue from sales is more than the expenses the business must bear). Your goal isn't to eliminate entropy completely (you can't). Your goal is to keep integration higher than entropy. The bigger the spread, the more potential for success your business has.

Keep in mind that when an organization has a high amount of internal entropy but temporarily gets more energy through sales, raising capital, or acquiring another company, this usually only compounds the underlying problems. If you've ever been part of a bad merger or acquisition, you'll know what I mean. Trying to bypass internal entropy needs is like trying to cure an illness by masking the symptoms with medication. Yes, it can feel better—but if the underlying condition is still there, you've got a bigger lingering problem destroying the system from within. For example, when you're tired (entropy) at work, you go and get a cup of coffee. This is a temporary stimulant to get you through the day. However, if you keep going for coffee again and again, the internal entropy needs are simply being masked, not solved. Ultimately, the acidity eats away at your health and your doctor recommends you quit the coffee, take up herbal tea, and get more rest and exercise to better manage your stress. Similarly, if you can solve the underlying conditions that are causing entropy to increase in your business, you'll roll more energy to the bottom line and have a stronger, more resilient, and high-performing organization.

Where Are Your Energy Drains?

Most popular business books and programs focus on increasing integration, usually through finding the right business or product strategy. Strategy is indeed critically important, as we'll see in Part III. Yet what gets too little attention is the havoc that high entropy plays on a system. It truly is the ultimate killer. In other words, entropy trumps everything else. If there's anything you should be doing in your business that you're probably not focused on enough, it's cultivating an awareness of entropy and a process to reduce it.

Personally, I didn't appreciate the significance of entropy in my own business until I ran into it. Hard.

In 1998, at the age of 28, I co-founded an affiliate marketing company in Minnesota and moved it to Santa Barbara, California. By 2001, the company was soaring like a rocket, generating incredible growth rates, and increasing staff and customers as fast as we could to scale. During this period, everyone who associated with the company, from the staff to the customers and even people on the street, seemed genuinely blown away by its energetic, passionate, and committed culture.

As co-founder and CEO, I would often walk into the office and feel lifted two feet off the floor by the collective energy and enthusiasm. I had installed a giant train whistle on the wall that the sales team would blow every time there was a sale. While the bankers on the second floor weren't too happy with the frequent "blaaaaaasssssssssstttttttt" of the whistle, we would all cheer loudly. It was a heady and intoxicating time.

Most of us had a feeling that the company had a growing opportunity in front of it and that we had the capabilities to execute on it. It was also relatively easy to make and implement decisions and there was a lot of momentum overall. That all seemed to change in a heartbeat.

During that heady period, I made the decision to hire a professional management team to supplement my own inexperience. "We're growing really fast and we need experienced hands to help us navigate," I said. But within two weeks of hiring the "pros," I walked on that same office floor and, rather than feeling uplifted, I felt a crushing weight. Rather than excitement, momentum, and progress, there was a palpable sense of fear, finger pointing, and infighting in the air. The new leadership had assumed a top-down approach, with closed-door decision-making that quickly eroded the culture we had worked so hard to build.

That extraordinary climate and momentum were gone. The friction within the system had become so high that the ability to maintain the system, make decisions, and get work done were greatly diminished. I was dumbfounded, confused, and afraid. "What is going on and how do I fix it?" I asked myself. I didn't know it then but I had run up against the classic laws of physics. I did understand, however, that if I didn't fix it fast, my company was going to fail.

Thankfully, this mini-crisis was a wake-up call. With some outstanding guidance, I was able to realign the organization, reduce the internal entropy, and accelerate its performance. Today, the company is the world's largest affiliate marketing company, CJ.com. If we hadn't dealt with the growing entropy, it would have been just another startup failure.

Sniffing Out the Drains

Now that you're aware of the basic principles behind success, make it a habit to regularly sniff out and eliminate energy drains in your life and work. Energy drains are a symptom of entropy. Energy gains are a symptom of integration. Your goal is to keep the gains high and the drains low.

Energy flows from inside out so begin with you. How's your physical, mental, and emotional health? Any energy drains? If so, what is causing them and how can you address them? Then, move outward to your primary love relationship and key family relationships. How are they? Is there friction or flow? If there's friction, what is causing it and how might you address it? Keep moving outward and look at your company. Where does energy seem to be flowing and where are the energy drains occurring? You do this by walking around, observing, asking questions, and listening. When you notice signs of unhealthy entropy, take note. Flow is good. Excessive friction is bad. Remember: Your company has a fixed amount of energy and whenever there's a real drain, it's stealing from your top-line performance.

For example, you may notice that there seem to be good flow and momentum in the sales process. You can tell because you have satisfied, paying clients who come back and buy more of your product or service. The sales team is motivated and working well together. At the same time, you might notice significant friction and energy drains within engineering. What's causing this? Is it the people? The process? The structure? A misalignment in vision and values? Whatever the cause, if you want to increase execution speed, you'll first need to address the drains.

Sometimes energy drains are so significant that they can seem impossible to handle. Maybe the friction with your board is so extreme that trying to address it seems more costly than putting up with it. Or perhaps you've lost trust and respect with your co-founder. How do you deal with something that, if it goes badly, could bankrupt the whole company?

Obviously, life is complicated and each situation is unique. I'm not going to insult your intelligence by telling you that there's a simple, magical, three-step formula to eliminate every major drain. But change always begins with a shift in perspective. And it's that greater perspective of the real cost of energy drains and their adverse impact on the system that I'd like you to cultivate. Once you begin to view problems and conflicts as energy drains, you'll be able to find energy-gaining solutions much more easily.

How you deal with energy drains and maximize top-line integration is the art and science of Organizational Physics. As you study and apply these principles to your life, work, and relationships, your ability to solve even the most complicated challenges gets better and better. For now, just remember that if you want greater top-line performance, you'll need to start by identifying the energy drains standing in the way.

If my focus on energy drains seems depressing, I'd ask you to reconsider. It's true that we each have a finite amount of time and energy to perform integration within our lives, to understand ourselves and others, and to experience the fullness that life has to offer. The inexorable pull of entropy, dissolution, and ultimately death is always present in the background. Even so, we are evolving beings with an impulse to create, integrate, and thrive. As Vaclav Havel so eloquently put it, "Just as the constant increase of entropy is the basic law of the universe, so it is the basic law of life to be ever more highly structured and to struggle against entropy."[3] When we manage the dynamic between entropy and integration with awareness and the right balance, that's when we meet our potential to be successful beyond expectation.

---

[3] Letter to former president of Czechoslovakia Dr. Gustáv Husák, April 8, 1975.

Lex Sisney

2. Where's My Satisfaction?

Are you happy in your job? The data says you're probably not. I can also speak from experience. For most of my life, I operated under a false assumption that the more successful I became, the more happiness I'd feel. But what I found was just the opposite. At one point in my early thirties, I had the experience of attaining everything I had once dreamed of. But instead of feeling elated and happy, I felt burdened, stressed, and beaten down by constant and competing demands. In my experience in the Young President's Association, a worldwide group of successful CEOs, I found that very few were actually genuinely happy as well.

Why is this? Why doesn't greater success seem to lead to greater happiness? There's an interesting study on success and happiness by Dr. Vance Caesar of the Caesar Group that sheds some light on this phenomenon[4]. In an ongoing study of high achievers (the top 2-3 percent of individuals in a given field) across all walks of life, Dr. Caesar discovered this: Only 1 out of 10 high achievers (.2 to .3 percent of the total pool) rate themselves as authentically happy. Imagine that: If you gather ten thousand top achievers from all walks of life—the rich, the famous, the talented—only a handful will actually consider themselves happy.

What's the difference between a happy high achiever and the rest? In his research, Dr. Caesar identifies eight attributes that dictate both success and happiness. Most of these are fairly easy to recognize and intuitively make sense. They include a driving sense of purpose, a compelling vision, and the intrinsic feeling that your work is meaningful. Other attributes include beliefs and behaviors that create inner peace, a regular process involving the three Rs (review, renewal, and recommitment), and outstanding discipline. Additionally, happy high achievers generally work with mentors and coaches.

It turns out that one of the secrets of the top of the top—the tiny fraction that is both successful and happy—is that they mastered the game of energy management to such a point that they *get more than they give from all of their key relationships*. That may sound confusing at first so allow me to explain.

As we've discussed, everything is a system and every system exists in relationship to other systems. What happy high achievers recognize is that everything in life is ultimately an exchange of energy. After our health, the single greatest factor that energizes us or depletes us is the quality of our

---

[4] Young Presidents' Association Forum Lecture, Santa Maria, California (April 18, 2009).

closest relationships. If you've ever been in a "vampire" relationship that sucks all the energy out of you, you know it can take days to recover from even a brief encounter. On the other hand, if you have a best friend who always seems to make you feel better, then even a brief encounter can float you higher for days. Recognizing this, happy high achievers make a conscious effort to establish and nurture energizing relationships.

Successful relationships are a two-way street. In an ineffective relationship, one or both parties experience the feeling of giving more energy than they get back. For example, a marriage where one partner feels she is constantly giving more than getting creates resentment. Over time, that resentment builds up and she says, "I'm leaving you because my needs aren't being met." In a business setting, the employee who feels he is continually giving more to the company than he is getting in return will soon become bitter and burned out, with either an ulcer or a new job search on the horizon.

On the other hand, a highly effective relationship is one where both parties are able to give each other what they need in a way that adds to their own energy. For example, a marriage where it's easy (i.e., there is a low cost of energy) for both partners to meet the needs of the other and both partners feel their needs are met is a highly successful union. The relationship "just works." In a business setting, you'll find a great mutual fit when an employee feels she is getting more from her job than giving to it, and her managers feel they are getting more from her than they're giving in total compensation. The employee is thinking, "I can't believe they pay me to do this. I would do it for free . . . can you believe it?" Similarly, her managers are thinking, "She is one of our top performers. She's passionate about what she does and delivers outstanding work. I wish I had ten more like her." The bottom line is that the relationship is net additive, supportive, and energizing to both parties. It just works.

The key differentiator, then, between happy high achievers and the rest is that happy high achievers are extremely vigilant about only allowing relationships into their lives that add to their energy. This includes their marriages as well as their relationships with their families, companies, boards of directors, key staff, and important clients. They make it a point to only allow relationships that are net additive. If a relationship isn't net additive, it's no longer one of their primary relationships. It gets shifted or it is gone.

Are You Giving More than You Get in Return?

The notion of getting more energy than you give from your key relationships can be a hard one for successful, driven people to embrace.

It's especially hard for entrepreneurs in the heat of battle to even fathom. How will a company that's cost so much blood, sweat, tears, and capital ever pay back more than its cost? But making this shift from energy-costing to energy-adding is not only the key to greater happiness, it's also the key to successfully scaling a business. Let me share a story to explain why.

A few weeks ago, I had lunch with a thirty-something entrepreneur and CEO. He runs a medical device company with revenues of about $10M. As we got talking, I learned a little about his history. He had started the business six years prior and fought through incredible challenges and turmoil surrounding his team, the market, and the investors. Like many entrepreneurs, he is in significant debt and double mortgaged on his home because every spare penny goes to the business.

Like every good entrepreneur and CEO, he was incredibly determined and willing to fight it out to make things work. But I could also tell that he was feeling worn down, beaten up, and resentful from the constant grind. His plan was to raise some more capital, get the company to profitability, and sell it off to a strategic acquirer. Then he could "take some time off, rebuild my marriage, and figure out what I want to do next," he said.

Even though I knew he didn't have the answer yet, I asked him, "Imagine you do sell the company. What do you think you'll do next?" "I know I should know this," he replied, "but I haven't got a clue. Something where I can start fresh and this time . . . do things the right way." "OK," I said, "I get that. But let me ask you another question. If you were able to run your current company, extract yourself from the things that cost you energy, and spend 80 percent of the time doing things that you love to do and are good at, would you still sell the business?"

"I'm not sure," he said. "On the one hand, I'd really enjoy doing that kind of strategic business development. I know that I'm at a point where I need to be working on the business rather than in it, but I just haven't been able to make the leap. On the other hand, my wife hates how much I work. She's terrified of how much equity we have tied up in the business. She wants less risk, not more. The current board is a pain in the ass to manage. It's like herding cats and I'm sick of it. It just seems easier to start fresh, with a clean slate."

I share this dialogue because most entrepreneurs (me included) have fallen into this trap at some stage. You fight so hard, work so long, take so much risk, and give so much to the business, that you end up ruing the day you started it. Trapped in a prison of your own making, the only exit you can envision is to sell the thing off and be free of it. You tell yourself that if you just fight it out long enough and find a buyer, not only will you have a big pay day, but you'll be free of everything. Pesky clients, irritating staff members, that board member you've wanted to tell off, the grind, the travel, the risk, the fear, the headache and hassle. And then, if you're creative and visionary, it seems so easy to spot new opportunities and launch a new business—something clean and fresh without all the baggage of the current one.

But here's the thing: The dream of scaling and selling a burdensome business to start fresh is just that—a dream. It's a folly, a myth, an opiate we use in hope of a brighter future. The reality is that if your business or career is a burden now, it's going to be very hard to create enough new energy to make it scale if you haven't lowered the entropy first. It's just physics. When entropy is high in the system, integration will be low.

If you truly want to be successful and grow your business, then you need to follow the principles of energy management. Rather than focusing on fighting through the friction and burden of your company, you'll want to focus on shifting the company so that it's no longer a burden to you now. That is, you'll need to shift your role in the company so that it becomes net-additive to you. Then use that new available energy to work on the business, rather than in the business, and allow it to scale.

A business is an asset, much like a car. If you had a car that wasn't working well—if it was a liability costing you more than the value you got out of it—naturally you'd try to sell it. Paradoxically, the best time to sell a car or any other asset is when you don't need to—in other words, when it's working great and you're getting a lot more back from it than you put into it. This is equally true for your business. If you're continually giving more to it then you get in return, then of course you're going to want to sell it. But if the business is an energy drain for you, it's going to be seen as an energy drain for a potential buyer as well. Who wants to buy a cheap, broken car?

Fortunately, unlike a car, your business has the potential for perpetual renewal, continually adapting to new market conditions and generating value and satisfaction for everyone involved. Ultimately, the act of freeing yourself from energy-draining relationships and activities in the business gives energy back to you. You can then use that new energy to create more energy-adding relationships and pursue those business activities that really light you up. If managed well, these relationships and activities will increase the enterprise value of your company and provide new energy and capabilities for it to scale.

How do you free up enough new energy to experience greater satisfaction and productivity across the board, along with greater business success? The art and science of Organizational Physics offers some powerful answers including how you build and manage your teams, choose the right strategy, avoid strategic pitfalls, and execute fast. But it starts even before that. It starts with your own recognition that if you want the business to scale, you can't keep doing what you've always done. You need to commit to a new mindset and new behaviors that support a new reality.

The good news is that the new mindset and behaviors support what you're naturally good at and energized by. That is, I'm not asking you to become someone you're not or spend more time in activities that cost you energy. Quite the opposite! I'm asking you to shift into more of who you authentically are and to play from your natural strengths—or in other words, from your genius zone.

Working in Your Genius Zone

A powerful way to conceptualize your energy gains and drains is to understand your personal genius zone. While few people are intellectual geniuses, each of us has an area of outstanding ability that allows us to perform at a high level and adds to our overall energy and satisfaction. This zone of activity is what I call the genius zone.

When you're operating from within your genius zone, you experience high energy gains. You tend to feel deep engagement, high personal satisfaction, and elevated productivity. You also produce outstanding work. When you're operating outside of your genius zone, you experience the exact opposite.

The secret to having greater satisfaction while growing your business is to align the activities of your own genius zone with the activities that simultaneously add the most enterprise value to the company. If you can get this mix right (and I'll show you how), that's when you'll experience that rare and intoxicating blend of genuine success and satisfaction.

Take a moment and reflect on this question: On average, how much of your work time is currently spent operating from within your genius zone? 10 percent, 30 percent, 80 percent, or more?

What I've found in my coaching practice is that, if you're personally spending 80 percent or more of your time working in your genius zone, then you are usually quite productive and happy in your work. If you're operating outside of your genius zone most of the time, then you're suffering from lower productivity, greater stress, and dissatisfaction. The bigger the gap, the greater your desire to make a change.

If you're constantly running from one mini-crisis to another in your work, then it may take a bit of introspection to get a sense of what activities actually represent your genius zone. If you'd like to explore this further, you can do it easily by writing down your answers to the following:

1. Allow yourself to recall a past activity or project in which you really excelled and that felt really good to do. Perhaps you lost track of time and felt energy and passion coursing through your veins. It may even have felt like you weren't "doing" anything at all. What talents were you expressing during this project or activity? Write down the three to five talents.

2. A good friend who knows you really well shares his or her appreciation of you: "You are so talented at _____!" What would s/he tell you? Write down another three to five talents.

Now, to get a sense of the talents within your genius zone, reflect on both lists of talents and choose the top three that most add to your energy and satisfaction while you're engaged in them. This may seem overly simple, but that's exactly the point. You don't have to go searching long and far to find your genius zone. Once you do, you just need to create an environment where you can express more of it in both your work and personal life—which brings us to understanding your vector of happiness and productivity.

The Vector of Happiness and Productivity

While lowering energy drains, increasing energy gains, and spending time in your genius zone are the foundation of a happy and fulfilled life, one final element allows you to experience the *highest* levels of satisfaction and productivity across the board. I call this element your "vector of happiness and productivity." Using this concept to reflect on your life can help you express your genius zone more fully in all areas of your life.

There is a simple model that can help you visualize what this means. Its basic concept was developed by Dr. Ichak Adizes, who created a Venn diagram mapping dimensions of personal experience that he calls "Is," "Want," and "Should." I've represented these dimensions below as "How you are," "How you want to be," and "How others want you to be," respectively:

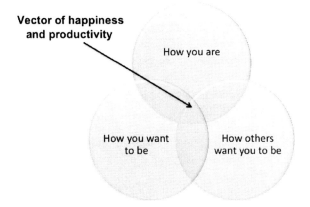

Figure 6. The Vector of Happiness and Productivity.

"How you are" refers to how you currently spend most of your time and energy. Think of it as how you "show up" in the environment. "How you want to be" indicates how you'd prefer to spend your time and energy. "How others want you to be" indicates the demands and expectations others in your environment place on you. The closer the alignment or overlap among these three dimensions, the less internal and external conflict you will experience, the greater the opportunity to work in your genius zone, and the greater the integration with your external environment. In other words, the vector of happiness and productivity brings it all together.

Conversely, when there's a significant gap among the three dimensions, there's likely a personal energy loss that results in lower happiness and productivity:

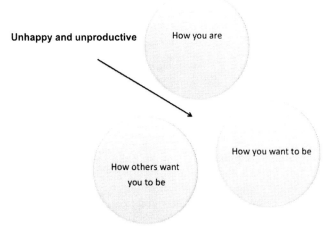

Figure 7. The greater the gap, the more unhappy and unproductive you are.

Let's see how this works. Imagine that you prefer to be innovative and creative in your work and consider yourself to be damn good at that. For a variety of reasons, however, you've been forced to show up each day bringing stability and structure to the company. In a nutshell, rather than being creative and visionary, you're forced to focus on the details and bring order out of chaos. What happens? Despite the fact that you're putting on a brave face and doing your best, you're also becoming burned out and the work is a struggle. In essence, it's costing you more energy than you get in return. Sure, you can do this for a time. But if it continues for too long, you'll try to find an escape that more closely aligns with what you truly want to do.

For the highest level of internal and external alignment, however, it's not enough to only do work you *want* to do. This is because no one operates independently of his or her environment. You also have to feel that you're meeting the needs of others, or how others want you to be. Understandably, if you feel that your environment is telling you to operate differently than how you are or want to be, this will create energy drains and stymie your productivity and happiness. You will therefore need to either work towards a newfound alignment with your current environment or find a new environment where you can be both authentic *and* thrive.

Your goal, therefore, is to create as little gap as possible among the three dimensions, which looks like a version of this:

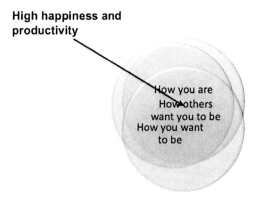

High happiness and productivity

How you are
How others want you to be
How you want to be

Figure 8. The narrower the gap, the greater the happiness and productivity.

So how do you accomplish all of this? How can you spend most of your time in highly productive activities that add to your energy and joy and simultaneously meet the needs of your growing business? How do you reduce the energy drains that are occurring across your business today—within you, the team, the company, and its operations—and maximize its gains?

While every situation is unique, the solution always lies in first understanding what's really going on—learning to recognize and work with the universal laws that operate within your team, strategy, and execution. Once you understand the principles, then you can deploy the right tactics. The rest of this book will show you how.

Part II - Build and Manage Powerhouse Teams

3. The Secret to Managing Everything

If you were to ask 1,000 people "What makes a good manager?" you'd get just as many different answers: "A good manager is participative and democratic." "No, a good manager is firm and decisive." "Actually, it's a person who listens really well but isn't afraid to make tough decisions." "It's someone who can manage the details and make the trains run on time." "A good manager is a visionary, can spot opportunities, and get others to act on them." "A good manager produces results." You get the idea.

If you were to read the most cited management literature, you'd see that there are myriad definitions and some confusion about what constitutes good management (participative, autocratic, etc.) and how varying approaches have evolved over time. In many ways, the differences in interpretation make sense. Many of them have to do with context—the time, setting, and surrounding conditions that impact what it means to manage and do it well. There's also the obvious fact that human beings are complex individuals attempting to manage complex situations. Naturally, each of us must attempt to deal with our complicated selves, others, and situations with limited resources and awareness.

But what if you could work with a universal theory of management that lays a foundation for all the rest? A theory that defines certain underlying principles of all human endeavors and interactions and could really explain what it means to manage anything? Like a talented engineer works at the underlying causes of an engine's performance, such a theory would help you work at the underlying causes of organizational behavior and manage its performance too.

In this part, you will learn how you can work with a singular, meta-level management theory that is simple, effective, and all-encompassing in its scope. This framework governs and explains the behavior of all organizations—from individuals and families to corporations. In fact, all aspects of organizational management can be understood through this lens, including the tasks being performed, the styles of the people involved, the behavior of subgroups, and even how the organization relates to its environment.

Think about that for a moment. This one theory explains all the rest. It's universal. It applies equally to a team in Bangalore and one in New York. It applies to your marriage and it applies to your management style. In the following chapters, I will explain how it works and show you how to use it simply and effectively. With a little practice, you'll find that your skills as a manager of anything will improve and lead to much better outcomes for you across the board.

Once you know the principles, you can look at any aspect of an organization—from the actions of the individuals involved to the performance of an entire company in the marketplace—and understand how it got to be that way. You will also be able to anticipate its future behavior and work with the underlying causes to change that behavior. This meta-model is powerful, pervasive, and universal.

The secret to understanding management is this: Complex adaptive systems (such as people and organizations) must (1) shape and respond to changes in the environment and (2) do so with a focus on the whole, as well as the parts and sub-parts of the system. If they are unable to do so, they will cease to get new energy from the environment and they will perish.

Intuitively, this makes sense. For example, imagine a family of four. If the family is to survive and flourish, it must shape the environment by getting resources such as money, food, and shelter. It must also respond to the environment, including changes that are societal, economic, ecological, and so on. At the same time, it must pay attention to all the parts that make up the family system—things like cooking, cleaning, commuting, paying the bills, and taking the kids to school. It must take into account the different and often conflicting needs of the individual family members. It must also give focus to holistic dynamics so that the family acts like a single, unified whole—for example, making sure that there's a sense of family identity as well as plenty of love, warmth, laughter, and nurturing for all of its members.

If the family isn't able to shape or respond to the environment, or if it loses focus on the parts or the whole, it will quickly run into trouble. If the pattern continues, then the family will disintegrate. Just imagine a family that doesn't have income, or is unable to perform its daily routine, or can't respond to economic changes, or whose members are always fighting with each other. Obviously, it's not a family you'd want to be a part of. It is not resilient or adaptive to change. Being part of the family costs all of its members more energy than they get in return. Such a family is on the verge of failure.

The same is true for every organization. It must be constantly shaping and responding to change while focused on the parts and the whole. I am, therefore, going to classify observable behavior, at its most basic level, as either *shaping* or *responding* to change while focusing on the *whole* organization or on its *parts* and sub-parts. I call this the *Adaptive Systems Model* of organizational behavior.

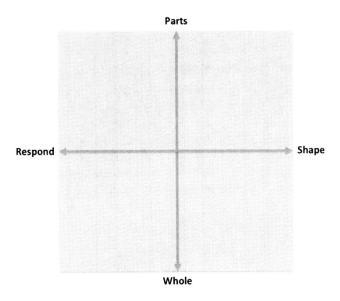

Figure 9. The Adaptive Systems Model provides a universal framework for understanding individual and collective behavior.

The dimensions of behavior within the Adaptive Systems Model exist on a relative and time-dependent scale. For example, if there's a high drive to shape the environment, then at the same time, there will be a lower drive to respond to change. If there's a high drive to focus on the parts, there will be a lower drive to focus on the whole. You can see this in your own life. Notice that, when the daily pressures and actions of your life consume you, you're not simultaneously focused on the big picture. That's why you periodically "get away from it all," go on vacation, or take time out to get a new perspective. Notice too that if you're busy building a new business, you don't have the time and energy to respond to all the little vicissitudes of life, family, friends, and so on. As the proverbial farmer would say, "There's a season to sow and a season to reap and they don't happen at the same time."

All behavior can be viewed and understood through this basic model. Note that I'm not talking about "good" or "bad" behavior, nor about why something is behaving the way it is—only that it is behaving along these relative dimensions.

Now that you have an overview of the basic dimensions of behavior, you can use this framework to reveal some amazing insights into the people and situations you're attempting to manage and do it more effectively.

The Four Forces of Organizational Physics

Using the Adaptive Systems Model as a guide, we can see that the behavior of any complex adaptive system—an individual, a team, or a company—can be broken down into four basic types or forces. I call these the Producing, Stabilizing, Innovating, and Unifying forces.[5] These forces coexist along a continuum that we can map on two axes, representing the drive to shape or respond to the environment and the drive to focus on the parts or the whole organization.

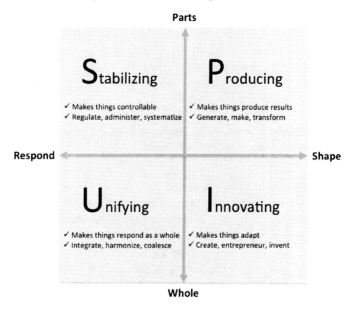

Figure 10. The four forces of Organizational Physics.

The Producing force demonstrates a drive to shape the environment and is focused on individual components or aspects of the system. The

[5] I originally learned the concept of four managerial codes from Dr. Ichak Adizes of the Adizes Institute, who uses the terms "Producing," "Administering," "Entrepreneuring," and "Integrating." While the central concept behind each code is the same, the Organizational Physics model introduces a more universally applicable terminology and performs a meta-level contextualization by coding each function based on its shaping or responding to the environment and focusing on the parts or the whole. Organizational Physics also differs significantly by integrating concepts from physics, evolution, and complex adaptive systems theory. For more on the Adizes approach to styles, see *Management/Mismanagement Styles* (Santa Barbara: Adizes Institute Publishing, 2004).

Producing force is what makes things produce results. Synonyms are "generate," "make," and "transform." Within a business, this is the drive to generate tangible results such as making the sale, completing the code, and getting the work done.

The Stabilizing force demonstrates a need to respond to changes in the environment and is focused on individual components of the system. The Stabilizing force is what makes things controllable. Synonyms are "regulate," "administer," and "systematize." Within a business, this force shows up as the ability to systematize the work being performed, including a drive to create greater efficiencies, improve quality, or reduce liabilities.

The Innovating force demonstrates a drive to shape the environment and is focused on the whole system. The Innovating force is what makes things adapt. Synonyms are "create," "entrepreneur," and "invent." Within a business, this is the ability to sense and act on new opportunities, to be disruptive of the status quo, and to anticipate and adapt successfully to change. You'll notice this strongly in entrepreneurial endeavors, new product development, R&D, and strategy.

The Unifying force demonstrates a need to respond to changes in the environment and is focused on the entire system. The Unifying force is what makes things respond as a whole. Synonyms are "integrate," "harmonize," and "coalesce." Within a business, this force shows up as the need to create teamwork, interpersonal connections, and a sound group culture.

With a little practice, you can begin to see the Producing, Stabilizing, Innovating, and Unifying forces just about everywhere you look. That is, the four forces are scale-independent. You can spot them from the macro to the micro, including within tasks, functions, individual behavioral styles, and your entire organization. Let's take a look and see how the four forces behave in a similar fashion at all levels of an organization.

At the macro level, the four forces dictate the behavior of how a business performs in the marketplace. A high-tech startup requires a very high Innovating force to disrupt the market and a Producing force to build the product. Compare this to a senior citizens' home. This needs a very high Stabilizing force to make sure that processes and regimes are followed and a high Unifying force to help the residents feel like they're part of a community.

As you dive deeper into how an organization functions, you'll see the same four forces at work. R&D requires a high Innovating force. Sales needs a high Producing force to win accounts. Accounting needs a high Stabilizing force to limit liabilities and focus on every dollar and penny. A high Unifying force is needed to keep the staff working together as one team.

Because a company is really just a collection of the people involved, you'll also begin to spot the same four forces within the styles of individuals doing the work. Ideally, the CEO needs to make sure the business is Producing results, Innovating for market demands, and Unifying the team around a consistent vision and values. A good account manager will express a high Unifying force in order to connect well with clients. A good accountant will have a high Stabilizing force that makes it easy to keep the books in order. A good entrepreneur will have a high Innovating force to spot opportunities, as well as a high Producing force to take action.

Even work tasks themselves can be understood through the four forces. For example, the product development process needs good throughput (Producing force), attention to detail (Stabilizing force), and strong teamwork (Unifying force). The strategy process needs high creativity (Innovating force). The controller process needs attention to detail (Stabilizing force).

The four forces are always at work within an organization. However, not all forces are present in equal amounts. Rather, the four forces exist in *co-op-etition*. They must cooperate because, without all four, the organization would quickly cease to exist. They must also compete for available energy and, when one force is consuming most of the available energy, this naturally leaves less for the others. This play of forces is what drives observable behavior and shows up in patterns that we'll explore in the coming pages.

From Forces to Styles

Each of us expresses a certain style—understood in its broadest sense as a mode of operating in the world—that reflects our own unique combination of the Producing, Stabilizing, Innovating, and Unifying forces. All four forces are present in each of us in some form, but usually one or two of them come to us most naturally. In addition, when one force is relatively strong, one or more of the other forces will be relatively weak.

While we may modify our general style depending on circumstances, stepping out of our natural strengths costs us more energy than operating within them. For example, imagine a highly innovative entrepreneur who is forced to do bookkeeping for a week. Sure, she may be able to do it, but she's also going to feel extreme tedium, effort, and a loss of energy as a result. It's because of this energy cost that most of us express fairly consistent characteristics that reflect our usual way of managing. Effective management, therefore, requires understanding your own style and its relative strengths and weakness, as well as that of the people with whom you work and interact.

The chart below shows how each basic management style compares to the others. It compares the pace (slow to fast) of how a style tends to act, think, and speak; the timeframe (short view to long view) of how a style tends to perceive a situation, trend, or idea; the orientation (process-oriented to results-oriented) of how a style tends to relate to people and situations; and the approach (structured to unstructured) of how a style tends to operate in daily tasks.

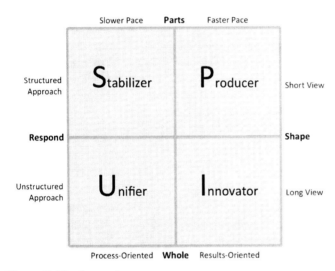

Figure 11. The four styles.

The Producer

The Producer (P) has a high drive to shape the environment and is focused on the parts that make up the system. Thus, this style moves at a fast pace, takes a short-term view, is results-oriented, and follows a structured approach. The Producer is focused on what to do now and working hard to get it done quickly. To get an immediate sense of the Producer's qualities, think of a fast-charging, focused, determined, high-energy person who thrives on working long and hard. That's a Producer.

The Stabilizer

The Stabilizer (S) has a high drive to respond to the environment and is focused on the parts that make up the system. Therefore, this style moves at a slower pace, takes a short-term view, is process-oriented, and follows a structured approach. The Stabilizer is focused on how to do things and working methodically to get them done the right way. To get an immediate sense of the Stabilizer's qualities, think of a very structured, process-oriented person who likes to analyze the data before making a decision. This person is highly organized, has outstanding attention to details, and takes their time in their words and actions. That's a Stabilizer.

The Innovator

The Innovator (I) has a high drive to shape the environment and is focused on the whole system. Consequently, this style moves at a fast pace and is results-oriented like the Producing Force, but takes a long view and operates in an unstructured way. The Innovator is focused on driving change while finding new and better ways of doing things. The lens they use to view the world is, "Why not?" as in: "Why not do it this way?" or "Why not try putting these two things together?" To get an intuitive sense of the Innovator's qualities, think of a dynamic, creative, big-picture person who has myriad new ideas and is usually excited by the latest one—until a new one strikes again. That's an Innovator.

The Unifier

The Unifier (U) has a high drive to respond to the environment and is focused on the whole system. Therefore, a Unifier moves at a more measured pace and is process-oriented like the Stabilizer, but takes an unstructured, freewheeling approach and a long view of change like the Innovator. The Unifier is primarily focused on who is involved and the interpersonal dynamics of the group. To get an immediate sense of the Unifier's qualities, think of a very likeable, gregarious, warm, people person who is in tune with others. That's a Unifier.

A Note About Language: When a person or organizational function has, or requires, a strong Producing Force, it is referred to as a "Producer" or "P." A strong Stabilizing Force is referred to as a "Stabilizer" or "S." A strong Innovating Force, an "Innovator" or "I." A strong Unifying Force, a "Unifier" or "U." As a mnemonic aid, think "PS I love U" and you'll remember the four forces: PSIU. In addition, strong and weak forces are distinguished by capital and lowercase letters, respectively. For example, a strong Producer is written: Psiu. A strong Innovator is written: psIu. A person or role that has or requires a strong Producer and Stabilizer is written: PSiu. And so on. This nomenclature is in recognition that every system needs all four forces and that not all four forces exist in balance.

Friends vs. Foes | Gains vs. Drains

One way to intuitively grasp the basic characteristics of each style is to recognize who it tends to view as friends (those they admire, respect, and value) versus foes (those they devalue, discount, or disrespect) as well as what tends to cost it energy (emotional drains like stress, anxiety, frustration, etc.) versus give it more energy (emotional gains like satisfaction, happiness, and confidence).

	Lens	Energy Drains	Energy Gains	Foes	Friends
Producer	What	Not enough time	Momentum/ results	Not working hard/fast	Working hard/ fast
Stabilizer	How	Not enough control	Order/ accuracy	Not doing it right	Follow the process
Innovator	Why not?	Too many ideas	Enthusiasm/ buy-in	Not getting it	Support their ideas
Unifier	Who	Too many conflicts	Harmony/ intimacy	Not working as a team	Add to the group

Figure 12. The friends, foes, gains, and drains for each style.

The Producer views the world as *what* to do. The energy drains for a Producer are the feeling of not having enough time to accomplish all of the work. And guess what? Producers always have too much work to do. In addition, it is their own internal clock that determines when work should be accomplished. The energy gains happen when Producers have a feeling of momentum and achieving results in their tasks and goals. Producers tend to like others who work as hard and as fast as they do and dislike people who don't.

The Stabilizer views the world as *how* to do things. The energy drains for Stabilizers occur when they don't feel they have control over a situation. They experience energy gains like confidence and happiness when things are orderly and accurate. Not surprisingly, Stabilizers like others who are accurate and thorough and dislike those who are not.

Innovators view the world as possibility. They ask, "why not?" The energy drains for an Innovator are having too many ideas to pursue. This may seem counter-intuitive because Innovators love ideas. When they generate too many ideas, however, they can't find their way out of a paper bag. The gains for an Innovator occur when one of their ideas takes hold and really works. Innovators like people who give them support. This could be as simple as excitement and encouragement for their latest idea or support from investors and employees who buy into their vision. Innovators dislike people who don't support their ideas.

The Unifier views the world from the perspective of who is involved. Because Unifiers value harmony in the system, they experience energy drains when there is too much conflict and gains when everyone is on the same page and working well together. The friends are those who add to the team chemistry and interpersonal dynamics. The foes are those who create conflict and destroy harmony in the system.

Meshing of Styles

Most mature, healthy adults aren't extreme versions of a singular style. Instead, they exhibit a range of styles depending on their current life conditions and level of development. In my experience, people generally seem to start out with one or two primary styles, can develop a third over time, and are usually weakest in one style throughout their lives. For example, if you were born with a high drive and high creativity, your style is PsIu. If you've learned to develop your stabilizing qualities over time through the demands of your school or work, you might show up as a PSIu. However, you've always been an introvert and enjoy alone time, so the U is the weakest of your styles. No amount of personal or professional development is going to change that relative balance.

Because all four forces compete for a finite amount of energy, if you are born a P and have matured into a U, that will mean that one of the other styles has backed off in predominance over time. For instance, I have a successful friend who was a PsIu (a typical entrepreneur style) for much of his career. He built and sold several companies. He's mellowed and matured over time. Today, he shows up more like a psIU. He's friendly, gregarious, creative, and loves to mentor others. That is, as his U qualities developed over time, his P qualities lessened. It would take tremendous energy and effort for him to reengage his former P qualities to do another start-up.

As you learn to identify the forces, you'll notice some common patterns emerging among different career types. Here are some examples:

Entrepreneur. Good entrepreneurs have an ability to see the future and act to make it happen (PsIu). They have a very developed innovator capability that allows them to see and anticipate how trends will converge in the future. They're not just visionary, however; they also have the willingness and drive to take action on that vision and produce results to make it happen. Because of this, as the company grows, a great challenge for most entrepreneurs is when and how to shift out of working *in* the business to working *on* the business.

CEO. If an entrepreneur is going to evolve into a CEO, then they'll need to develop either their S (PSIu) and be a shrewd and calculated operator or develop their U (PsIU) and be a visionary who can rally a larger company and market to their cause. There's a popular notion among management circles today about the difference between a "wartime" and a "peacetime" CEO. The basic difference is that, in a time of crisis, contraction, or "war," a company needs a CEO who can analyze the situation, make a bold decision, and be ruthless in execution (PSIu). In times of expansion and growth, or "peace," however, the company needs a CEO who can build bridges, form alliances, and find new growth opportunities, all while executing on the quarterly goals (PsIU).

Implementer. An implementer (PSiu) is someone who can work really hard and be highly organized. You'll find them thriving in tasks that require effectiveness and efficiency in high-pressure situations. If this person wants to evolve their career, they can develop their U (PSiU) and become an Operator or a person who can drive results, manage the details, and coalesce a team—very valuable skills for a chief operating officer.

Sales person. A good sales person has a high drive to produce results and thrives on winning (Psiu). However, you'll meet many different styles of sales people. There's the PsiU who is a great sales manager because they walk the talk and coalesce the entire sales team. There's the PSiu who is outstanding at working hard, producing accurate contracts, and creating and following a scalable sales process. Compare this to a good client relationship manager who should demonstrate pSiU in that they can follow a process, keep the client on track, and have great interpersonal relationships at the same time.

Engineer. Engineers come in many different types. If your organization uses traditional waterfall engineering, then you'll want an engineer who can work hard and follow the documentation and standards (PSiu). However, if you use an agile methodology, then you'll want an engineer who works hard and is a great team member (PsiU) or is highly creative (PsIu) while following a sound agile process that provides the S for the team to follow. A good code for a scrum master would be (PSiU). In this case, they work hard and gain the respect of the team (P), create and follow a sound process (S), and keep everyone on the same page (U).

The Cause of Different Styles

So what is the cause of different styles? Why does one person act differently than another in any given situation? Obviously there are many factors that influence why a person behaves a certain way. There's genetics, environmental factors, personal history, family history, education, culture, and more. But there's one fundamental element that plays a key role in conjunction with all these factors: energy.

Here's why. As I discussed in Part I, every system (person, organization, etc.) operates with a finite amount of energy. We conserve our available energy to maintain ourselves, make decisions, and get work done. In order to survive and flourish, we must get new energy from the environment—just as you must get oxygen from the air while reading this or a business must get new revenues from its clients in the marketplace. This quest for new energy compels us to shape and respond to the environment and to do so while focusing on the whole, as well as the parts and sub-parts. If not, our system will cease to get new energy from the environment and it will perish.

In an attempt to make the most efficient use of our available energy, we develop habits. Our habits are unconscious patterns that govern how we interact with the world. When we're dealing with a lot of change, for example, it generally costs us more energy to manage. When we can make our actions into habits, we have more energy available to attempt to be in integration with the outside world. That's why professional athletes practice for hours on end—so that the perfect swing becomes second nature. They don't have to think about it. It costs less energy.

Our style, therefore, is formed over time and becomes a habit because it is how we learned to cost-effectively shape and respond to the world while managing all of the parts and sub-parts that make up the totality of our systems. That's why Producers tend to get more energy by working hard and feel stymied when obstacles are in their path. That's why Stabilizers tend to get more energy by creating order out of chaos and feel overwhelmed when there's not enough control. That's why Innovators prefer to drive change—it gives them energy—and why they feel drained when others don't enthusiastically support their latest ideas. And it's why Unifiers like to maintain harmony and low conflict—it costs them less energy than disharmony and high conflict.

Identifying the four forces not only allows you to quickly discern what's really happening; it also helps you gain self-awareness and better accept yourself, others, and the situations around you. At the same time, it improves your ability to orchestrate win-win situations by giving whatever you're managing what it really needs. And this will make your life a lot easier, more satisfying, and even more fun.

How to Manage It All

With different forces all around, deep inside your organization and far outside in the market and your life, how can you possibly manage it all? Managing organizations and people can often seem chaotic, challenging, and frustrating. Crises and disorder can strike at any moment. Especially in fast-growing companies, management actually feels like operating in permanent white water. You just do your best to keep your head above water and not sink. Still, the four forces show us that there is order in apparent chaos—and when you have a sense of the underlying forces involved within a person, team, task, or situation, you gain a profound awareness and can respond more astutely.

As I mentioned earlier, the term "management" means different things to different people. Depending on who you ask, management sometimes means controlling, administering, leading, inspiring, overseeing, and so on. Plus there are the many different styles of management—autocratic, democratic, participative, data-driven, instinct-driven, visionary, practical, disciplinarian, laissez-faire, etc. The answer to "What is management?" usually depends on context, including time, culture, situation, and experience. But what is management, really?

The simple answer is: *Management is the application of force.*

By "force" I, of course, don't mean coercion, compulsion, or pressure but rather the application of the Producing, Stabilizing, Innovating, and Unifying forces. In short, to manage it all, you need to understand and use the appropriate force for a given situation. This is determined by many factors, encompassing both strategy and execution, which we'll investigate further in the following pages. However, there's one general rule of thumb for better management: Identify the force behind what you want to manage.

If you understand the makeup of forces behind what you want to manage, then you can work at the underlying causes of behavior. Spotting the forces isn't hard at all. With a little practice, you can begin to quickly break down any behavior into its component forces and become a much better manager as a result.

This principle of management is the same whether you're managing a little league team or a Fortune 500 firm. For example, imagine that you're a little league baseball coach. It's the first day of practice. The kids show up and they're eager to play. How do you get the best out of the team and create a positive experience for everyone involved, including yourself? According to this model, the first thing you do is identify the forces behind what you want to manage. Here's how it works.

Begin with you. What type of baseball coach are you? Are you a strong Producer who leads by example and exhorts the team to play harder? Are you a strong Stabilizer who excels at planning a well-run practice schedule by the numbers? Are you a strong Innovator who finds creative ways to manage the game, train the players, and create breakthroughs? Or are you a strong Unifier who excels at creating a strong team spirit and all-for-one-one-for-all mentality?

Of course you have all of these dimensions to your personality but, if you look closely, you'll see you're exceptional at certain things and, when you're engaged with them, you experience greater energy, joy, and satisfaction. Other tasks cost you more energy than you experience in return. Perhaps you love to speak in front of the team and share the innovative strategy to win each game but the act of putting together a daily practice schedule is not your strong suit. In this case, it indicates that you're a stronger Innovator and weaker Stabilizer and so you'll want an assistant coach who can complement you where you're weaker and s/he is stronger.

As you and the assistant coaches execute your season, you'll need to make sure that there's the right balance of forces working within the team throughout. The ultimate goal of the team is to get more runs than the opposition and win enough games to win the pennant (Producing force). In order to do that, you'll need to ensure that the players understand the rules of the game and each knows the basics of their stance, swing, position, and situational awareness (Stabilizing force). You'll also want to engage in activities that build team unity and ensure that the boys are playing well together (Unifying force). As the team progresses in the basics, you'll need to add new training techniques, more advanced and creative playmaking, and new strategies based on the increasing skills and awareness of the team (Innovating force). All four complementary forces are necessary to win the pennant.

When you break things down into forces, it becomes faster and easier to see what the team really needs and give it to them. Let's say that the team is winning games. This could mean that the Producing force is really high and the game is performing at a high level. But it could also mean that the competition is lousy and your team has gotten lucky. Which is it? Perhaps you notice that the team is getting cocky and there's fighting among the players. Over time, this could negatively impact the team's ability to win. In this case, you'll want to increase the Unifying force by finding ways to create a team-first mentality. Or let's say that the team isn't winning games, the practice schedule is a mess, there's no organization or discipline, and things are rapidly falling apart. In this case, you'll want to reassert the Stabilizing force to bring some order and discipline to the situation. Once that's in place, you can look for quick victories to rebuild the Producing force by focusing on hits, outs, solid playmaking, and wins. If it's a long season and the players are losing their enthusiasm, you'll need to amp up the Innovating force to keep things interesting and cutting-edge for the players.

Throughout the season, you'll want to assess the forces behind the individual players and coaches too. What are they dealing with and where do they need training and support? For example, little Bobby has high energy, can't sit still, and swings wildly at each pitch. You recognize that you'll have to give him some extra attention to focus on the task at hand (Producing) and to develop a strong stance and technique (Stabilizing). If he can develop those forces, he'll be a good player and so you resolve to coach him in those areas. On the other hand, little Fernando has got a natural swing. He is focused and loves to win (Producer), is a natural leader, and makes everybody on the team a better player (Unifier). In order to coach Fernando, you know that you've got to build a trusting bond with him first because Unifiers tend to need that deep interpersonal connection in order to thrive. If you can establish that with him, Fernando can help you build a strong sense of team and enjoy a great season.

Depending on which forces are balanced or imbalanced, you will need to adjust your coaching style and the focus of each practice. If you amp up the wrong force or apply forces in the wrong sequence, you'll have a big mess on your hands just as if you allow the necessary and needed force to diminish. For example, if the team is winning games and playing well, the Producing force is doing just fine. But what force should you give the team next? It depends. You won't want to amp up the Producing force so high that the team burns out. Nor will you want to amp up the Stabilizing force so high that things get too rigid and no one is having fun. Nor can you go crazy on the Innovating force by constantly throwing new information and strategies at the team without their first having integrated past lessons. They'll just feel confused and their faith in you as a manager will falter. You also can't allow the Unifying force to get so extreme that politicking, infighting, and backstabbing take over. The team needs to be unified to such an extent that it helps them be resilient but not so inwardly focused that they lose sight of winning the game.

There's a time and a place for everything and understanding what force to apply as well as how much, when, and in what sequence, comes from knowledge and experience. In other parts, I discuss how to execute on any given strategy by understanding where the organization is in its lifecycle and then giving the organization the forces it needs to progress to the next stage.

For now, it's enough to keep this in mind: The art and science of management is recognizing the forces at work within a system and adjusting them along the way. Ineffective management is just the opposite. It occurs when the wrong force, the wrong amount of force, the wrong sequence, or the wrong timing are applied. When this happens repeatedly and systemically, an organization will fail. And notice that there are many more ways for things to go wrong than right! (Yes, entropy is always at work).

By the way, the terms "right" and "wrong" are not value judgments but physics statements. If you step hard on an upturned rake in the grass, the handle will hit you in the face. It's not right or wrong to step on a rake but the result is predictable. If you keep stepping on the rake, you'll keep getting hit in the face. Effective managers will work with—not against—the laws of physics. This means, first of all, understanding the forces and patterns in front of you. Then you can look at any aspect of your organization—from the actions of individuals to the company's performance in the marketplace—and understand how it got to be that way, anticipate its future behavior, and steer that very behavior towards greater integration and success. This is the art and science of great management.

4. The Producer Style

T he Producer has a high drive to shape the environment and is focused on the parts. Thus, it moves at fast pace, takes a short-term view, is results-oriented, and follows a structured approach. The Producer is focused on what to do now and working hard to get it done rapidly. To get an immediate sense of the Producer's qualities, think of a fast-charging, focused, determined, high-energy person who thrives on working long and hard. That's a Producer. If you put this person in a rowboat and say "Row!" what will they do? Well, they'll just start rowing straight ahead—and fast! They don't need to ask questions, plan a route, understand where they should go, or even how long they'll be gone. They just row and keep rowing until you say "Stop!"

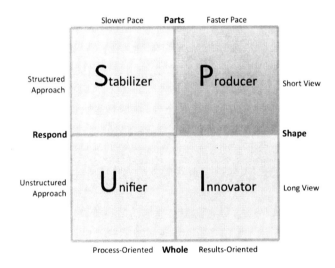

Figure 13. The Producer style.

The Producer has a tremendous capacity to work hard to accomplish a goal and takes great pride in winning. That could be winning the new account, completing the project, achieving an objective, or beating the competition. A Producer is decisive and makes decisions based on what can be accomplished now, without waiting for all the information to be in hand. Instead, they figure it out as they go. Our best Producer qualities are our ability to act, lead the charge, overcome obstacles, urge a team to action, and be effective, assertive, and victorious. A Producer is a lot like the engine of a car. The bigger the engine, the faster the organization can go.

The Big P

When the Producer trait is exceedingly strong, we call it a Big P. A Big P is like a hammer. It sees every problem as a nail and the solution is to hit it. Hit it with hard work, more work, and faster work. The Big P comes into work very early and leaves work very late. If they have an office, it's likely very messy with lots of projects and tasks to complete (and usually awards and trophies on display). The Big P doesn't like to have meetings unless they're short, to the point, and focused on the most pressing task at hand. Their biggest frustration is that things aren't getting done fast enough according to their own internal clock. Their common complaint is that others aren't working as hard as they do. Their answer to most problems is to work harder, longer, and faster. Because of this, they tend to overestimate the amount of work that can be accomplished by a team. Therefore, when getting schedule estimates from a Big P, recognize that they are going to significantly underestimate the actual time it will take to complete a team project. If they say one month, it will be more like three to four months.

The Big P can't stomach falsity and they're often brutally honesty in their communication. If you went into their office, the first thing you'd hear about is how hard they've been working and how much they still have to complete. When this person supervises others, there's a lot of anxious waiting by the staff because the Big P is not very effective at delegating. Often, they delegate at the very end of a project when they just can't do the work themselves and a deadline is approaching fast. The staff then leaps into action to try to solve another last-minute crisis.

The reason that the Big P always has so much work to do is because they value themselves and others based on how much they do. Delegating tasks or planning ahead to avoid a crisis actually decreases the Big P's sense of self-worth. The Big P thrives on averting crises. And the bigger the crisis, the better. In fact, sometimes the only way you can get their attention is to present a new crisis for them to fix.

Big P Under Stress

When the Big P is under extreme stress, they tend to become erratic in their actions. They will tend to make a lot of mistakes because they can't see the big picture, understand the details, or communicate and unify the rest of the organization. It's the classic "Fire, ready, aim!" When angry, the Big P tends to lash out verbally, tell others what to do, and become domineering or aggressive.

Big P and Other Styles

Big Ps get along really well with other Producers because they value hard work and move at the same fast pace. They don't mind Stabilizers as long as the Stabilizers don't create "unnecessary" barriers to getting work done. But if they do, watch out. Producers respect an Innovator's ability to see into the future but dislike Innovators who cause too much chaos or changes in strategy because that requires Producers to refocus and change their work. That's hard for a Big P to do. Producers will often judge Unifiers as sycophants who don't do any real work, chitchat all day, and play the political winds—unless, of course, a Unifier can help the Producer alleviate obstacles that are in the way of getting tasks completed. In that case, they'll form an uneasy alliance.

Managing a Big P

If you're managing a Big P, you never have to worry about them working hard enough or finding the inner motivation to complete a challenging task. Instead, you need to be mindful that they don't run too far in the wrong direction. While another style might require the symbolic whip to trigger them into action, the Big P will need a set of reins to slow them down. A Big P needs a high level of autonomy in their tasks and the best way you can support them is to help eliminate obstacles that prevent the work from getting done. Also be mindful that, because the Big P is outstanding at completing the tasks at hand, they may have blind spots around how the work is impacting others, how the big picture has changed, and the intricate details involved. If you praise them for being productive and celebrate and honor their victories, you'll have a loyal employee.

If Your Boss is a Big P

If your boss is a Big P, you will need to demonstrate your value based on measurable achievements and how long and hard you work. That is, if you're working long and hard and producing tangible results such as sales wins, products launched, hours billed, or capital raised, then you'll be in good standing with your boss. If you need a request fulfilled, you better phrase it quickly and to the point and be able to show how it is necessary for completing short-term tasks and goals. The Big P values actions more than words and has little patience for politics, bureaucracy, or anyone and anything they view as standing in the way of what they want to achieve.

The Big P thinks and speaks literally. They are plain-spoken. A "yes" means just that and a "no" does too. Therefore, a Big P takes you at your word as well. If you say you'll do something, even in an off-hand way, they'll remember it and hold you to it. If you follow through, you'll be accepted and rewarded. If you fail, you'll lose favor with the Big P, regardless of the surrounding circumstances. The Big P loves to reward and promote for performance and to fire for a lack of performance. It's black and white. So when it's time to discuss your performance review, be prepared to validate your wins and state how you will mitigate your losses going forward. If you keep failing to hit your stated goals, you're at risk of getting fired, regardless of the circumstances.

In the 1992 movie *Glengarry Glenn Ross*, Alec Baldwin plays an extreme Big P. His character, Blake, is sent in by the faceless owners of a real estate office to motivate the salespeople. Blake shows up with a pair of brass balls, cusses out the sales team, and announces a contest where only the top two salespeople will get the more promising leads and everyone else will get fired. That's a Big P. Perform or else—and do it quickly.

Summary of the Producer Style

Producer qualities allow us to work hard, achieve our goals, and be decisive and effective in our actions. They provide the engine for accomplishment. When taken to an extreme, they turn into Big P—a giant hammer that only sees what's in front of it, gets overwhelmed by taking on too much, and seeks to alleviate its frustration by pushing things to go faster.

The Producer	
Enjoys	Completing tasks
Personal work space	Cluttered/busy
Normal communication style	Energetic/fast/to the point
Primary work focus	Implementing the game plan/producing output
Typical complaint	People aren't working hard enough
Decision making behavior	Quick/figures it out along the way
Addresses problems by	Working harder/getting others to work harder
Likes to be praised for	Being productive/working hard
Excels at	Taking action
Most satisfied when	Scores a victory

Figure 14. Traits of the Producer Style.

5. The Stabilizer Style

The Stabilizer has a high drive to respond to the environment and is focused on the parts. Therefore, this style moves at a slower pace, takes a short-term view, is process-oriented, and follows a structured approach. The Stabilizer is focused on *how* to do things and working methodically to get them done the right way. To get an immediate sense of the Stabilizer's qualities, think of a very structured, process-oriented person who likes to analyze the data before making a decision. This person is highly organized, has outstanding attention to detail, and takes their time in their words and actions. That's a Stabilizer. If you put this person in a rowboat and say "Row!" what will they do? Well, first they'll analyze the rowing mechanism and plan the most efficient stroke. Then they'll want to understand where they are rowing, for how long, what the best route is, when the water and food breaks will occur, and the prevailing winds and currents. Once everything is planned in detail, with two contingency plans in place, then they'll start to row!

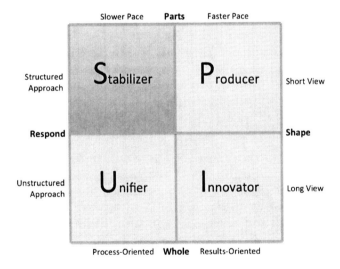

Figure 15. The Stabilizer style.

The Stabilizer has a tremendous ability to find better, more efficient ways of doing things. They excel at organizing, planning, controlling, and systematizing things. They create order out of chaos and usually have outstanding retention of pertinent details. The Stabilizer tends to value control over freewheeling innovation, unless that innovation can be analytically justified. They have little patience for errors, sloppiness, or anyone or anything violating a defined process or procedure without good cause. A Stabilizer is methodical and makes decisions based on analyzing the data and finding more efficient solutions. Naturally, it takes time to gather and analyze data and to understand the intricate details involved in a decision. Consequently, the Stabilizer moves at a deliberate pace in their thoughts, words, and actions.

The Big S

When the Stabilizer trait is overly high, we call it a Big S. A Big S is like a bureaucrat who seeks to control for change by establishing and following processes. They value efficiency over effectiveness, even to the extreme. The Big S comes into work on time and leaves on time. If they have an office, it's likely very clean and orderly with files neatly arranged and spreadsheets and objective data readily on hand. The Big S schedules regular meetings and always has an agenda prepared in advance. Their biggest frustration is that others aren't following the process. Their common complaint is that others don't pay close enough attention to important details.

The answer to most problems for a Big S is to analyze the data and document a plan. Because of this, they tend to falsely believe that proper planning can account for any contingency. Therefore, when getting schedule estimates from a Big S, recognize that the schedule will look excellent on paper. It will be very specific, down to each nut and bolt, but also totally incorrect because change is a constant. Consequently, there will likely be several creative ways to accomplish the same objective but much more quickly.

If you walk into their office, the first thing you might hear is how there's a need for more process and control. When this person supervises others, there are usually a lot of other Stabilizers on the team because the Big S values adherence to standards and protocols as a top priority. They delegate frequently and monitor the work being performed using project plans and milestone reviews. Unlike the Big P, a Big S can't manage a crisis well. There's too much noise and confusion for them to quickly and accurately get a read on the situation.

Big S Under Stress

The Big S must always plan due to a fear of lack of control. For them, a lack of control leads to bad things happening. Asking the Big S to move more quickly, be creative, or take a huge risk is asking them to face their biggest fear. When the Big S is under extreme stress, they tend to withdraw inwardly and focus on unimportant but controllable details. For example, in the classic movie *The Caine Mutiny*, Humphrey Boggart plays an extreme characterization of a Big S in the role of Captain Queeg. When under stress from a life-or-death naval crisis at sea, Captain Queeg could only resort to enforcing rules about the consumption of strawberries and his crew was forced to mutiny to survive.

Big S and Other Styles

The Big S gets along really well with other Stabilizers because they value process, control, and planning. They don't mind Producers as long as the Producer is not violating any procedures. But if they do, watch out. They distrust fly-by-the-seat-of-your-pants Innovators because Innovators have three new ideas per week, all of which cause more work and headaches for the Big S. They find Unifiers to require way more interpersonal connection and emotional support than they're willing to give, so they prefer to avoid them entirely. If avoidance isn't an option, they'll smile tightly and find an excuse to get back to their private office where they don't have to engage in intimate conversation.

Managing a Big S

If you're managing a Big S, you rarely have to worry about them making errors and omissions. Instead, you need to be alert that they don't fall into paralysis by analysis. A Big S needs lots of structure in their tasks and the best way you can support them is to give them the relevant data to analyze and then allow them time to process it. Be mindful also that, because the Stabilizer is outstanding at understanding the details, they may have blind spots around how the work is impacting others, how the big picture has changed and thus impacts the work being performed, and the real effort involved in executing the plan. If you praise them for being accurate and thorough, you'll have a grateful employee.

If Your Boss is a Big S

If your boss is a Big S, don't expect a warm open door policy but do expect a highly controlled and efficient work environment. If you have a need or a request to make, expect to hear "no" a lot since it's hard for a Big S to say "yes." This is because they tend to need a lot of information and time to analyze an issue before committing to a course of action. Therefore, a "no" from a Big S is more like a "not yet, I need more information." Even if you get a "no" from a Big S, you can usually return with more information and revisit the decision later. Once you get a "yes" from a Big S, you can take it to the bank. It's very unlikely that they'll change their mind.

The best way to get a Big S to take action is to point out how something is violating an existing policy. If you can do that, mountains will move. If not, the next best course of action is to point out how the new decision will improve efficiency for the organization. Don't try to appeal using your personal needs or by pursuing an innovative risk. For example, if you need a raise, don't say, "My husband lost his job and we can't afford to pay the bills." That's a personal appeal and it will fail. Instead say, "According to HR Policy 254, Level 1 employees shall be rewarded per annum by 5 percent." And then make a case that, based upon your job duties, you actually should be reclassified as a Level 2 and thus earn a higher salary.

Summary of the Stabilizer Style

Stabilizer qualities allow us to be accurate, secure, and efficient. They permit a factual, deliberate, and methodical approach to planning and decision making and create a sense of order out of chaos. They promote high quality and follow-through. They also help us to be cautious, thoughtful, and prudent when faced with the unknown. When taken to an extreme, a Big S becomes a liability, however, by always valuing efficiency, even at the cost of effectiveness, and risking paralysis by analysis.

The Stabilizer	
Enjoys	Analyzing problems and tasks
Personal work space	Practical/organized
Normal communication style	Factual/deliberate/methodical
Primary work focus	Planning/organizing/systematizing
Typical complaint	People not following the process
Decision making behavior	Methodical/decides once everything is understood
Addresses problems by	Implementing new systems/revising policies and procedures
Likes to be praised for	Finding efficiencies/creating order/high quality
Excels at	Analysis
Most satisfied when	Achieving high quality

Figure 16. Traits of the Stabilizer Style.

6. The Innovator Style

The Innovator has a high drive to shape the environment and is focused on the whole. Consequently, this style moves at a fast pace and is results-oriented like the Producer, but takes a long view and operates in an unstructured way. The Innovator is focused on driving change while finding new and better ways of doing things. To get an intuitive sense of the Innovator's qualities, think of a dynamic, creative, big-picture person who has a plethora of new ideas and is usually excited by the latest one, until a new one strikes again. If you put this person in a rowboat and say "Row!" what will they do? Well, they'll start to come up with new ideas! "Why don't we put a sail on this baby? How about a glass bottom? Come to think of it, a 250hp motor would do just the trick; I bet we can find one at the marina. Be right back."

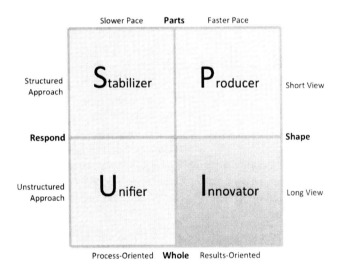

Figure 17. The Innovator style.

The Innovator has a tremendous ability to peer into the future and anticipate how seemingly disparate trends will (or can be made to) merge together. They are highly conceptual and easily get excited about new ideas and opportunities. Because an Innovator can sense change occurring faster than other styles, they spend a lot of time trying to get others to see the same thing they do. They usually attempt to do that by explaining the idea and sharing their enthusiasm, and by trying to get others to understand and be enthusiastic too. Our best Innovator qualities are our ability to anticipate change, to be imaginative, charismatic, and inventive.

Without the Innovator force, we would have no ability to adapt to changes in our environment and we would quickly become irrelevant or extinct.

The Big I

When the Innovator trait is exceedingly strong, we call it a Big I. A Big I is like a mad genius. It's always cooking up one crazy-sounding idea after the next. The Big I comes into work whenever they want and leaves work whenever they want. If they have an office, it's likely a testament to their own unique individuality and creativity. The Big I doesn't like to have meetings unless it's to discuss a new idea and as long as they get to do most of the talking. Their biggest frustration is that things are stymied in production and implementation or that they get bogged down in managing release schedules and milestone dates, rather than working on the next new thing. Their common complaint is that others "don't get it." Their answer to most problems is to come up with a new idea.

The Big I is not usually comfortable giving schedule estimates because they recognize they just don't have any interest in (or clue about) how long something will actually take. Those are details for others to figure out. They are happy, however, to give predictions on when market trends will converge. At the same time, because they see the future (not necessarily the accurate future) so clearly, they tend to overestimate when something will actually occur. Therefore, if they think the market demand will tap out in two years, in reality it will probably just be getting started then. If and when demand finally does arrive, the Big I is already bored with it—"OMG, that's so last decade!"—and has moved on to yet uncharted territory.

The Big I gets bored with the status quo really easily. Their past creations are never good enough because something new keeps being invented. If there's nothing new to build or think about, they prefer to destroy what's already been built. "Hey, let's tear this old thing down and rebuild something new." When you walk into their office, the first thing you'll hear about is their latest idea and why it's important and revolutionary. When this person supervises others, there's a lot of chaos among the staff, projects, and schedules. They'll usually have a right-hand person who suffers while trying to keep up with the extreme amount of innovation and who has learned to distinguish a passing notion from a true need for implementation.

The reason that the Big I always pursues so many different ideas and opportunities is that they're afraid of standing still and being trapped. Standing still means risking boredom and there's not much more terrifying than that. So to ask a Big I to focus on one thing and complete it is like asking a crack addict to put down the crack pipe. It's very, very hard and not much fun at all.

Big I Under Stress

When the Big I is under extreme stress, they tend to think themselves into a corner. Because they see so many options, it's hard to choose one. Thus, they'll want the flow of options and counter options to stop so that they can pick a path and get out of the mess they've created. The Big I tends to seek escape when under duress. So if things are going poorly in the office, you can expect to find them thinking of a new idea, dreaming of a vacation or a fun new purchase, diving into entertainment, or generally trying to avoid reality. When angry, the Big I can get very volatile and hypercritical of others.

Big I and Other Styles

The Big I appreciates Producers because they act really quickly to implement their vision. However, sometimes it can be frustrating to have to explain to the Producers why the Big I is changing the strategy again. "Can't they see it? It's so obvious!" Besides, to a Big I, Producers are kind of boring and uncreative. They absolutely dislike Stabilizers who are finicky, slow, and say "no" a lot. They distrust other Innovators and view them as arrogant competition. They enjoy Unifiers because they are easy to be around, always have a supportive and encouraging word for their latest idea, and can be useful allies in galvanizing support for their vision.

Managing a Big I

If you're managing a Big I, you have an outstanding idea generator and a terrible implementer. If you have a good relationship, they'll want to bounce new ideas off you frequently because they need to talk things through and weigh different possibilities. Often they can be scattered and inconsistent so you'll need to make sure that the work is actually getting done and that the details are being managed well. Because the Big I is capable of generating so many new ideas, they are often unaware of how the changes they propose are hard for everyone else to keep up with. They overlook the intricate details involved in implementation and conveniently forget all of the half-completed projects they've left in their wake. If you praise the Big I for having great ideas and get excited about them, you'll have a loyal employee.

If Your Boss is a Big I

If your boss is a Big I, you will need to demonstrate your value by helping them complete the pieces of the puzzle they see in their mind. Whatever you do, though, don't add to or change the vision for them. That would be like taking their paintbrush and drawing on their half-completed canvas. It's very risky and the Big I may never forgive you for it. Instead, ask questions, gently point out gaps in the planning, and always try to be enthusiastic about their ideas. Because a Big I changes their mind so frequently, you'll need to be able to discern between a passing notion and real action item. "Oh that, we're not doing that any more; I changed my mind this morning. Didn't I tell you? Here's what we're doing now . . . " is something you'll hear frequently.

The Big I thinks and speaks conceptually in big patterns and generalities. They see things others just can't. They promote people who they believe can help them achieve their vision. They fire people who no longer fit the vision or who seem to be creating obstacles to achieving it. If they are away on a long airline flight, you can expect them to show up at the office with a list of fifty new ideas and improvements.

In general, the Big I has a hard time saying "no" to interesting new ideas or appealing opportunities. If you present a proposal to a Big I, however, you might get a "yes" or a "no" depending on how your idea fits or competes with their own vision of how things should or could be. If they say "no", it's usually because your proposal doesn't align with their own version of the current vision. But unlike a Big S, you can't go back and try again. That's it. It's over, unless the Big I can begin to see how your proposal fits into their vision. A "yes," on the other hand, doesn't really mean "yes." It is more like "sure, sounds pretty good, let's explore it more." For example, if you were to ask a Big I, "Mr. Jones, what do you think about this new prototype?" and Mr. Jones responds, "Hey, I like it! Very cool! We could also make it do this…" That's not a legitimate go-ahead signal. When Mr. Jones comes back in two weeks and you show him the progress on the prototype, he'll probably say something like, "What? Why are you working on this? I didn't approve of this. It's time you focus on the XYZ project. We're already three months behind schedule!" So, a "no" is a final "no" from a Big I but a "yes" is more of a "maybe."

In the 1985 hit movie *Back to the Future*, Christopher Lloyd plays Doc, a madcap inventor and a pretty good depiction of a really Big I. He always seems to have three new ideas running through his head; he has a garage full of half-completed inventions; he's enthusiastic; he loves to think big; and the viewer is never quite sure if he's for real or insane because he's so far out there on the edge.

Summary of the Innovator Style

Innovator qualities are what allow us to sense and adapt to change and to find creative solutions and new opportunities. Innovators are creative and dynamic. They have an innate ability to see things others can't yet see. When taken to an extreme, the Innovator turns into a Big I and can become overzealous in pursuing too many different strategies, all half-baked and constantly changing.

The Innovator	
Enjoys	Spotting new opportunities
Personal work space	Unique/creative
Normal communication style	Charismatic/expressive/excitable
Primary work focus	Moving the next latest thing forward/spotting trends
Typical complaint	People aren't getting it
Decision making behavior	Bold/decides once the opportunity is sensed
Addresses problems by	Looking for new approaches or ideas
Likes to be praised for	Finding creative solutions that work/getting others excited
Excels at	Conceptualizing
Most satisfied when	Thinking outside the box

Figure 18. Traits of the Innovator Style.

7 . The Unifier Style

The Unifier has a high drive to respond to the environment and is focused on the whole. Therefore, a Unifier moves at a more measured pace and is process-oriented like the Stabilizer, but takes an unstructured, freewheeling approach and a long view of change like the Innovator. The Unifier is primarily focused on who is involved and the interpersonal dynamics of the group. To get an immediate sense of the Unifier's qualities, think of a very likeable, gregarious, warm people person. If you put this person in a rowboat and say "Row!" what will they do? Well, they'll want to know where everyone else is! You can't expect them to row all by themselves. They'll need a team of people, ideally their friends, to climb in the boat and all row together.

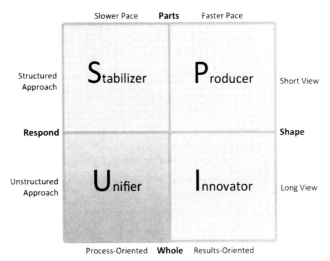

Figure 19. The Unifier style.

Unifiers are excellent communicators and team builders and are especially good at listening and empathizing. They tend to make everybody else feel uplifted, listened to, and respected and thus improve teamwork and loyalty in the workplace. They always have time for a chat and are genuinely concerned with how you are doing and how they can help you. They are excellent at smoothing things over and intuiting how someone else is really feeling. For example, if a Producer and a Unifier went on a sales call together, the Producer could only interpret what the client was actually *saying* while the Unifier could tell how the client was really *feeling* beneath the words. Our best Unifier qualities are our ability to create rapport, understand and motivate others, build cohesive teams, and create sound organizational cultures based on caring, empathy, and loyalty. Without the Unifier force, we would have no ability to respond to change efficiently because the organization couldn't act as a whole.

The Big U

When the Unifier trait is extreme, we call it a Big U. A Big U is like a politician who always seeks to curry favors and plays the political winds to their own advantage. On the one hand, they value and leverage personal relationships; on the other, their words can't be taken at face value because their loyalty will shift with the prevailing winds. The Big U comes to work when expected and leaves when expected. If they have an office, it's likely very warm and inviting and personable. The Big U likes to have meetings because it gives them a chance to see and connect with others and gauge which way they really stand on an issue. During the meeting, they prefer to sit and listen while others do the talking. Their biggest frustration is when others won't engage with them in a dialogue, shut them out, or keep up a stoic guard. Their common complaint is that others aren't working well together and thinking of the team.

The answer to most problems for a Big U is to gather input from others and process feelings (their own as well as others'). This takes time and that's why a Big U tends to move at a slower pace than a Producer or Innovator. Therefore, when getting schedule estimates from a Big U, recognize that before committing to any schedule, the Big U will insist on getting input and buy-in from those who will be impacted. The result will be a very safe, prudent schedule that will account for the needs of all the different constituents. Thus, there are likely several ways to improve the speed or direction of the plan if you're willing to step on some proverbial toes.

If you went into their office, the first thing a Big U would do is warmly invite you in, offer you some tea or coffee, and give you all the time in the world to be heard. When this person supervises others, there are usually a lot of other Unifiers on the team because the Big U values camaraderie and teamwork. They delegate frequently but don't tend to follow up too vigilantly because that can create conflict, something the Big U prefers to avoid.

Sometimes a Big I can appear as a big people person or a Big U. However, the Big I is really motivated to connect and influence people to move forward their own vision. When the time for selling the vision is through, a Big I will want to retire and be alone. For a Big U, however, being with people is a joy unto itself.

In the classic movie *The Godfather*, Michael Corleone's older brother

Fredo (whom Michael ultimately has killed in *The Godfather Part II*) plays the part of a Big U. Fredo is always seeking approval, wants to be liked, is trapped within his own feelings, and prefers to avoid conflict. It's hard for Fredo to take a stand so competing factions within the Mafia easily influence him. Ultimately, he betrays his family and justifies it because life has never been fair to him. That's a pretty good depiction of an extreme Big U. Nice enough, always wanting to get along, and yet underneath capable of being spineless, wishy-washy, and seeking power by currying favors.

Big U Under Stress

During a crisis, the Big U can fail to be decisive. There are too many conflicting viewpoints and hardened positions for a Big U to have the time to navigate. When under extreme duress, the Big U acts as if they're imploding under the weight of their own emotions. It's hard for them to see the big picture, do the work, make decisions, or even get out of bed. They'll need lots of time and companionship to process their emotions, restore their energy, and get reinvigorated.

Big U and Other Styles

The Big U gets along really well with all the other styles, especially those in power—all other styles, that is, except for other Big U's with political power! In this case, they can become highly suspicious and seek to either guardedly curry favor or quietly usurp the other Big U entirely. The Big U prefers to create a harmonious, low-conflict environment. But if they ever feel betrayed, they will rarely forgive the offender.

Managing a Big U

If you're managing a Big U, you will need to give them a lot of one-on-one attention and show that you care about them personally. Be aware that, because a Big U can be outstanding at helping a group work in harmony, they won't work as hard as a Producer, with as much attention to detail as a Stabilizer, or with as much creativity as an Innovator. If you share about your personal life, ask about their own, take them out to coffee or lunch, and give them praise and support, you'll have a loyal employee.

The best way to get a Big U to take action is to allow them to help you. Big U's love to help people who are important to them because they want those people to be happy and feel good about their relationship with the Big U! If you have a loyal Big U working for you, they can move mountains by opening doors and working their personal relationships.

If Your Boss is a Big U

If your boss is a Big U, expect to have a fun-loving, gregarious, lax work environment when things are good and a politically rife environment when things are not. Either way, who you know and who you're connected with are more important than what you accomplish. The Big U makes decisions based on personal likes and dislikes and on the prevailing political winds. When making a request, you can expect to hear "yes" and "no" a lot, but you can't take either one to the bank. This is because Unifiers tend to change their mind based on what others are thinking and feeling and who's in power at a given time. Therefore, a "no" from a Big U is more like a "maybe . . . could be . . . we'll have to see how it all plays out." And so is a "yes."

Summary of the Unifier Style

Unifier qualities are what allow us to be excellent connectors, communicators, and bonding agents for a group. They love to be with people, keep conflict low, and have a harmonious environment. When taken to an extreme, the Unifier morphs into a Big U and becomes a political animal, saying one thing and doing another to ensure their survival and advancement.

The Unifier	
Enjoys	Listening and empathizing with others
Personal work space	Warm/welcoming
Normal communication style	Appreciative/connecting/affirming
Primary work focus	Building consensus/meeting people's needs/teamwork
Typical complaint	People aren't being team players
Decision making behavior	Astute/decides once everyone's viewpoint is known
Addresses problems by	Communicating/bringing people together
Likes to be praised for	Understanding others/Uplifting the team/emotional intelligence
Excels at	Empathizing/unifying a group
Most satisfied when	Developing strong relationships

Figure 20. Traits of the Unifier Style.

8. The Key to High-Performing Teams

Growing up, I had a good friend whose dad was very successful. They lived in a gorgeous home on Lake Minnetonka where I was lucky to spend a lot of time, hanging out and enjoying their largesse. Among the things I vividly recall about their home was a refrigerator magnet that read, "Behind every successful man is a wise woman." I remember that magnet because it made my fourteen-year-old self wonder, "Hmmm, is Mrs. B trying to tell the world that she's equally responsible for all this magnificence?" and "Is it really true that all successful men have a supportive woman behind them?" or "Maybe it's her way of putting her husband in his place . . . " I didn't have the answers then but looking back, I can see that this message (dated and cliché as it is) is worth pondering and has implications for marriages and businesses alike.

Marriage or partnership is an exemplary opportunity to match and leverage complementary PSIU forces. No one can be predominantly change-driving, change-responding, focused on the parts, and focused on the whole all at the same time. For much of human history, sexual and gender differentiation resulted in men playing the part of PsIu while women played the part of pSiU. That is, men were responsible for bread-winning (P) and strategy or career advancement (I) while women were responsible for organizing domestic life (S) and taking care of children and family (U). In short, the left side of the PSIU chart shows the classic "feminine" functions and the right side the "masculine" ones.

In the United States in the 1970s, when baby boomers shifted to a dual-income family model and women entered the professional workforce *en masse*, women joined men on the Producer and Innovator (or traditionally "masculine") side of the chart. The result? Couples started outsourcing their Stabilizer functions to housekeepers, bookkeepers, and organizers and their Unifier functions to babysitters and marriage counselors—all to keep the family together!

Today, as many of us have outgrown long-standing assumptions about gender and marriage, we can see that the point is not about gender roles. Rather, it's that all four forces must be present for a family—however you define it—to thrive. Specifically, what all successful and harmonious unions have in common is that both partners naturally complement each other (or find alternative ways of bringing all four forces into the relationship). For example, a partner who is a balanced PsIu will tend to harmonize well with someone who is a balanced pSiU. If one partner is naturally externally focused on career innovation and the other is internally focused on domestic harmony and organization, the partnership can really work. If one partner is naturally better able to focus on short-run needs and structures, while the other is better at seeing the long run and creating harmony, that can also really work. Any number of themes and combinations are possible. What matters is that the partners bring in all complementary forces and (as long as they share love, trust, and respect) they can have a thriving partnership.

Compare that to a relationship where both partners are entirely focused on their careers and personal ambitions, while displaying strong Producer and Innovator traits (PsIu). If this occurs, there won't be enough force organizing and bonding together the family, which will suffer and tend to disintegrate. On the other hand, consider a union where both partners are stable and prudent but prefer to hang out with their friends than develop their careers (pSiU). In this case, the couple will probably have a great social life and terrible cash flow. It takes a complementary team to have a chance at a happy relationship—and both partners must give and take to create a balance.

If you shift the lens to organizational dynamics, you'll notice that a highly successful and visible business leader usually has a highly capable and less visible complementary partner. For example, Apple's late CEO Steve Jobs was recognized for his inventiveness, charisma, and uncanny ability to predict the future of technology and anticipate (even produce) consumers' desires. Jobs was also famous for his blistering attention to product detail. In one oft-repeated anecdote, we hear that Jobs ordered the original iPod dismantled the night before the press launch when he noticed that the headphone jack did not make a satisfying click when inserted. These are classic traits of the Innovator. Jobs was also infamous for his impatience and high work ethic. These are classic Producer characteristics. As a management style, therefore, Jobs coded as PsIu.

Tim Cook was Apple's COO (now CEO) who, according to most reports, was a perfect complement to Jobs. Cook works at a relentless pace (Producer), is a spreadsheet junkie with ruthless attention to detail on the supply chain (Stabilizer), and is also down to earth, soft-spoken, and good at maintaining relationships (Unifier). As a management style, therefore, Cook is a PSiU. Cook's production drive met Jobs' own. They both demonstrated extreme attention to detail, but in different domains. While Jobs was a powerful Innovator, Cook is more of a Stabilizer and Unifier who makes things efficient and smoothes the way with others. Together, they made a powerful complementary team.

According to a 2011 profile by the *New York Times*, "Their complementary skills have helped Apple pull off the most remarkable turnaround in American business, and made it the world's most valuable technology company."[6] The *Times* also recognized that a huge void would need to be filled when Jobs passed on: "When Mr. Cook is on his own, he will have to compensate for the absence of Mr. Jobs—and his inventiveness, charisma and uncanny ability to predict the future of technology and anticipate the wishes of consumers" (all Innovator qualities).

So while Steve Jobs was celebrated as the world's greatest CEO, behind the scenes he had a complementary partner and executive team. The necessity of the complementary team gets short shrift in the media, however, which celebrates the cult of the individual. Just browse through any bookstore and you'll see the mugs of Donald Trump, Bill Belichick, Jack Welch, Richard Branson, or the latest guru celebrated with very little mention of their complementary partners who supported their success.

Even business schools promote this cult of the individual leader. Read a popular business book about leadership and it will say something like this: A good leader produces results (P), brings efficiency and systems (S), is able to innovate for changing market demands (I), is a good people person (U), and focuses on the vision and values (U). This is nonsense. It's a myth. Just because it gets spun as fact in the media doesn't make it true. The bottom line is that if you want to be successful (and happy), you simply can't go it alone. It takes a complementary team to be successful.

Getting from PSIU to Really Good Management

You now know that there are four fundamental forces (PSIU) that shape individual and organizational behavior. You also know that these forces compete for available system energy and that if even one of the forces is absent, the organization will perish. I've also mentioned that, if you want your organization to do something new—such as change direction or accelerate performance—you must engage the appropriate force. But how does all this translate into practical steps? And how can you use it to be a better manager of people and situations?

1. Know the Forces at Play

Knowing the forces at play within an individual or an organization delivers fast insight into what otherwise appears as complex or random behavior. For example, if you set up a team with all Producers, then that team is going to demonstrate some predictable behavior and outcomes.

---

[6] Miguel Helft, "The Understudy Takes the Stage at Apple." *New York Times* (January, 24, 2011). Retrieved from http://www.nytimes.com/2011/01/24/technology/24cook.html.

It's going to move very quickly, produce a large volume of work, and blow past its milestones in record time. However, the work is going to have errors (it will be an inch deep and a mile wide), it will totally miss out on the implications and the coordination with other departments, and it will lack creative problem solving. A team of all Unifiers would have very different but equally predictable outcomes.

There's another important benefit to knowing the forces at play: It allows you to see and accept things for what they are, with less judgment. You should not underestimate the power of this. On the one hand, judgment is the capacity to assess situations or circumstances astutely and to draw sound conclusions. Obviously, good judgment is a critical skill for a manager. On the other hand, it's hard to be a good manager when you're holding personal judgment against someone or something. That type of judgment causes us to close down, stop seeing what's really there, and miss out on finding creative solutions. It also causes the other person (the person being judged) to feel resentful, unrecognized, and discounted. Like everyone else, I've experienced both sides of judgment, as both the judge and the judged. I can unequivocally say that interpersonal judgment demonstrates a lack of personal responsibility and results in a waste of energy and a loss of opportunity.

Growing up, my younger brother Carter and I fought constantly. I was the "responsible" older brother intent on working hard and "making it big" in the world (PsIu). He was the young, carefree spirit who loved to hang out with his friends (psiU). I'm ashamed to say that I would frequently nag, condemn, and ridicule him to get his act together, "be a man," and make something of himself. The truth is that my vision of him was severely clouded by my own judgment and he responded to me as you probably would: "F--- off. You're not in charge of me!" Later in college, after a few years of living apart, I took a road trip to visit him in Bozeman, Montana, to go hiking and camping in the mountains. In this new environment, and probably because I was out of my own comfort zone, I was able to let go of my "judgment vision" and see my brother in a whole new light. In fact, I was utterly in awe at what I saw. Here was a young man who was extremely capable, knowledgeable, thoughtful, and powerful. Who was this person? Where did he come from? The fact is that he was there all the time. It was my own judgment that had prevented me from seeing him fully. What a sad loss of time, brotherhood, and missed opportunity!

On the other hand, I've also been the judged when my boss couldn't truly hear, see, or listen to me without his own judgment vision clouding the interaction. For example, the man who taught me the most about organizational development is Dr. Ichak Adizes. He's a brilliant thinker, highly regarded and wise. Many rightfully refer to him as the Peter Drucker of his era. I was originally introduced to his work as an entrepreneur and we struck up a collaboration and a friendship. Later, because I was so enamored with his methods, I joined his organization as an associate. However, soon after he became my boss (and not just a friend and mentor), something really interesting happened.

He no longer seemed to see, hear, or understand me as clearly as he did before! On the receiving end, it felt like now there was a thick interference field operating between what I spoke and what he heard, between who I was and what he saw. Because I had the experience of collaborating with him deeply before he became my boss, the discrepancy was really profound. Now that I was "inside" the organization, it seemed that I was subjected to the same type of judgment vision I had projected onto my brother. As an employee, my own judgment vision towards him was equally activated. Now, there was no longer an individual and friend, but a "boss" and my own projections of whatever that entailed. All in all, we were two talented, capable people who couldn't see past their own judgments.

To be clear, I don't think my example of judgment vision between employee and boss is unique. In fact, I think it's the norm. For example, the COO for a famous personal development guru recently approached me seeking help around their growth strategy: "Lex, basically the guru doesn't listen to anyone inside the company. He really only listens to external experts. We're stuck on this issue and we need an external expert that he'll listen to." We all judge others and ourselves incorrectly. Sometimes consciously, usually not. It's good to be reminded that, while judgment of ourselves and others may sometimes feel right and good, it's really a loss of energy, productivity, and human potential. There is a better way.

Instead of letting your interpersonal judgments run wild, learn to judge the force, not the person. By "judging" or identifying the force, you are able to respond to the underlying energy patterns at work, without becoming caught up in personal criticism. You'll give yourself and others the freedom to be fully seen, heard, and reach full potential; you'll have more productivity and less drama in relationships; and your entire organization will have a greater chance to flourish.

Judging a force is pretty straightforward. Rather than labeling it as good or bad, right or wrong, you simply observe it in action. Is this individual or situation change-driving or change-responding? Are they dealing with the parts or with the whole? Is it a Producing, Stabilizing, Innovating, or Unifying force or some combination? And what force is most needed at this time? By identifying the force, you are better able to discern behavior without getting caught up in the drama. For example, if I had understood the force within my brother, "Oh, that's the Unifier force. It likes to connect with people and build relationships," then I'm sure our interactions wouldn't have been so needlessly draining for both of us. Similarly with my old boss, if I had learned to judge the force rather than the person, I would have been much more effective: "Ahhh, that's the Innovator/Stabilizer combo. I shouldn't offer up new ideas in this situation. Instead, I should ask some thoughtful questions to help him reveal his own vision further. And when I do see an opportunity to pursue, I should come prepared with lots of data to support it."

When we don't reduce others to the sum of our judgments, not only do we see more clearly but we also allow them to respond to us in a more positive way. We can then enjoy much healthier, more creative, and less energy-draining relationships.

2. Give the Force What It Needs

Each of the four styles has a particular focus and need. Producers are focused on what to do and need autonomy to do their work. Stabilizers are focused on how to do it and need time and data to perform analysis. Innovators are focused on finding new solutions and need excitement for their ideas. Unifiers are focused on the people involved and require time to process relationships and emotions.

Good management requires versatility. You don't manage different people or situations the same way. An effective manager is a flexible one who understands the different focus of each style and gives each one what it needs. Of course, to be truly flexible (and not just wishy-washy), you need to have a strong internal vision and values. You also need to know yourself. Are you a Producer, Stabilizer, Innovator, Unifier, or some combination? And what are your biases? Whatever your style, it impacts how you see the world and interact with others. Good managers recognize their own style and have the ability to adjust it for short periods based on those with whom they are interacting—all without compromising their own authentic vision and values.

Why is it important to meet the needs of each force? Assuming that you're dealing with a mature individual, as you give a force what it needs, the energy of that force "moves through" and can make space for the emergence of other forces. But if a force doesn't have its needs met, the energy stagnates and causes entropy to rise. Put another way, once someone has had their immediate needs met, they are in a much better state to be able to see and appreciate all the other forces and perspectives involved.

Imagine that you're sitting in your office and different styles of people are coming to you for advice. In the following examples, we are going to assume that you are a psiu—that is, you have an equal balance of all four forces. Of course, in real life, no one has a perfect balance so you will have to adjust your temporary style based on your predominant style. Here's how you might successfully interact with each style by giving each force what it needs.

Polly Producer storms into your office. She has high energy. She's talking fast and moving quickly. She's focused on what to do and is frustrated at the continued delays. Your task is to give the force what it needs. So what do you do? You speed up your pace. You take a structured approach. You focus on the most immediate short-term objectives. You help remove any obstacles that are preventing the work from getting done.

Once Polly Producer has had a chance to vent her frustration, she's once again able to focus on completing the task at hand. In addition, because you've met the immediate needs of her strong Producing force, Polly is now able to see things in a new light too. She can have a greater appreciation for all the details (Stabilizing), as well as an improved awareness of other people's perceptions (Unifying) and the big picture of the overall strategy (Innovating). You can now give Polly plenty of autonomy to complete the task. And because she's a Producer, you don't have to worry about the work getting done. You only have to check that it's the right work and she hasn't gone too far in one direction.

Sam Stabilizer knocks on your door. Sam speaks and moves at a more deliberate, thoughtful pace. He's focused on how to complete a task or project. He's in your office because the recent corporate objectives don't make perfect sense. So what do you do? You slow down your pace. You carve out time to really explain things. You give Sam all the information and raw data involved in the decision. You focus on the short-term practical issues. You help him focus on how to do things more efficiently. You give him plenty of time to analyze the data.

After Sam Stabilizer's needs are met, he can amp up his creativity (Innovator) and production power (Producer) and better connect with others (Unifier). But if Sam was never given the data or the time to analyze it, he would simply be stuck in his Stabilizing force. There's no sense in berating Sam to work harder, to be more creative, or to be a better team player until you've also given him time to analyze and make sense of the data. By doing this, you're able to leverage Sam's talents and will likely uncover aspects of the problem or situation that would remain hidden if he, or someone like him, hadn't analyzed it.

Isabel Innovator makes a grand appearance. She speaks and moves in broad, fast strokes. She's been thinking about the new project and has some ideas. "Why not do it this way?" she asks. So what do you do? You amp up your own pace and get excited! You give her the space to go really big picture and take an unstructured, creative approach. Together you explore the broader implications, and uncover where new innovations lie.

Once Isabel Innovator has had a chance to get excited with someone about her new idea, she may notice that the romance of it starts fading—followed by an increased awareness of the real effort (Producing), details (Stabilizing), and teamwork (Unifying) involved in bringing it to life. The result will be a better, more well-rounded decision. Isabel can now get out of her own way too. She can still be highly creative but won't be nearly as disruptive by always throwing new ideas into the mix just because they're new and she wants to be heard.

Ulysses Unifier enters your office and wants to chat. He's focused on who is doing the work on the new project and is noticing that team morale isn't has high as it could be. Ulysses moves, speaks, and thinks more deliberately and is usually "happy" and gregarious (unless he's upset and will then need time to process his feelings). In this case, Ulysses seems really upset. So what do you do? You slow down your pace and try to see the world as Ulysses sees it. You give him space to share his feelings and get his perspective on the needs of the rest of the team. You empathize with him.

After Ulysses Unifier has had a chance to process his feelings, he's much more capable of doing the work (Producing), following the process (Stabilizing), and supporting the new strategy (Innovating). If he doesn't get his Unifier needs met, he's going to be unproductive. Not only that: His gifts as a Unifier, including the ability to uplift others, empathize, intuit, and bring harmony to the team will be lost. By giving the force what it needs, the energy moves through and Ulysses can be at his best once again.

It's obviously hard work to give a force what it needs. It takes time, energy, skill, and awareness to do it successfully. But if you don't give a force what it needs, what happens? Our old enemy entropy starts to rear its ugly head. When the needs of a force aren't met, rather than dissipating, entropy increases and becomes detrimental to the individual and to the team.

Polly becomes frustrated to the breaking point. Sam withdraws into quiet resentment. Isabel gets dejected at the lack of interest around her and spins out even more crazy ideas (or stops sharing altogether). Ulysses gets so caught up in the melodrama that he becomes moody, grouchy, and petulant. So yes, while managing others well is hard and time-consuming work, not managing well has an even greater cost. Doing it right is always worth your time.

So far we've discussed that the elements to building and managing powerhouse teams lie in understanding the forces at work within a situation, team, or individual; forming complements of forces; and giving the system or force what it needs to be successful. Are these the only requirements for building powerhouse teams? Certainly not. Because the four forces are so pervasive, however, understanding them is a cornerstone to good management and team building.

There are other key elements to building powerhouse teams that are equally important. These include creating organizational alignment with the vision and values, designing the right organizational structure, having a sound process for decision-making and implementation, and hiring the right style of person for each organizational role. As you'll see in coming chapters, understanding the essence of the PSIU forces allows you to align all aspects of the organization, including your own role, with greater clarity and power. First, though, let's dive into how PSIU shows up in your strategy and business development.

Lex Sisney

Part III - Choose the Right Strategy

Lex Sisney

9. The Goal of Any Strategy

There are as many opinions about strategy as there are gurus pitching different approaches. "Gather customer feedback, do rapid iterations, test your assumptions." "Don't ask your customers because they can only tell you what they know. Instead, imagine what could be." "Get customer buy-in up front, then design the product." "It's a race and the fastest company wins." "Avoid the commodity trap." "Manage the innovator's dilemma by anticipating market changes." "Cross the chasm of practical buyers and then scale." "Harness the wisdom of the crowds for superior insights." "Leverage your core competencies and stick to your knitting." Usually, there's some great wisdom in each strategic philosophy and yet many camps provide conflicting advice.

What if there was a universal model for doing strategy? Something like an Über- or meta-strategic model that encompassed and made sense of all the rest? Such a model would shed considerable light on both the right and the wrong kind of strategy. It would explain why some companies seem to easily exploit a market opportunity and other companies struggle. It would give you a sequence of steps, provide indicators that you're on or off track, reveal pitfalls along the way, and provide a clear path to success. If the model was robust enough, it could account for conflicting advice from different strategic camps (at least the sound advice) and synthesize it into a cohesive whole.

I'm going to show you some universal principles that do just that and, from these, I'm going to give you a strategic model that is just as universal in its application. That is, a successful strategy follows these principles and a doomed one does not.

Once again, this model doesn't come from the ivory towers of Harvard Business School or even within the battlefields of the Fortune 100. Instead, it comes from evolutionary biology. In fact, Charles Darwin laid out the foundation for this Uber-strategy in his masterpiece *On the Origin of Species* (and no, it's not "survival of the fittest").[7]

Every potential business strategy has the same ultimate aim. This is true whether you are trying to sell your business, go IPO, enter a new market, raise venture capital, hire top-notch talent, fend off competitors, manage increasing regulations, win an industry award, or create the next hot startup. It doesn't matter what the strategy is—the goal is always the

---

[7] Charles Darwin, *On the Origin of Species by Means of Natural Selection: Or, The Preservation of Favored Races in the Struggle for Life* (New York: D. Appleton, 1864).

same. This goal is independent of time or context and it's always the same. It's just as true in recessionary times as it is in boom times. It was true one million years ago and it will be true one million years from now. So what is it? The ultimate goal of any strategy is *to acquire new energy from the surrounding environment now and in the future.*

The evidence for this comes from the most fundamental tenet of evolution: adaptation. Before we continue, let me clear something up about evolution. When most people think of evolution, they think of Darwin. And when people think of Darwin, they usually recall the term "survival of the fittest." However, Darwin himself never used that term. Well, that's mostly true … Darwin only used it late in life to refute the notion that success goes to those most fit. Instead, Darwin made clear that survival (and prosperity for that matter) is for those most adapted to their environment. If there's good adaptation or integration with the environment, then the species will flourish. But if the environment changes and the species can't adapt, it will fail. That's why *you're* reading this and not some brontosaurus.

What about survival of the fittest? This question comes up often enough that I want to address it now. Survival of the fittest is certainly important. It is a measure of how fit an organization's capabilities are in extracting available energy from opportunities in the environment. For example, imagine two leaders. One is an aboriginal chief in Australia. The other is an executive at Lehman Brothers. Who is the most fit? It depends on the environment. If the banker is stranded in the outback, there is lot of opportunity to survive and flourish but he just doesn't have the capability to execute. The aboriginal chief, on the other hand, can enjoy a good life if left in the wild because he's more fit for that environment. Back in New York, if the environment changes—for example, if there's a financial collapse—the banker's skills will no longer be useful and he or she will need to adapt to new conditions. Adaptation to the environment is supreme and fitness or capability is always secondary.

Why is adaptation with the environment so important? Because that's where new energy comes from. Without new energy, a system will perish. For example, if a man is stranded on a desert island, unless he can find new sources of energy like food and water, he's quickly going to die. Evolution shows us that if the environment has no more energy to give (if the resources are tapped out) and if the species can't adapt, it will fail. Or, if the species can no longer extract available energy from the environment and if it can't adapt, it will fail too. This will happen if its capabilities are no longer suited to the environment or the competition is too great relative to the size of the opportunity. In the same way, a business with no new sales will quickly die.

In Organizational Physics, "energy" is simply a measure of available or stored power. In a business, this is equivalent to all forms of available or stored power including money, resources, and market clout. Basically, a good definition of energy is anything useful and desirable that can be made productive. In fact, begin to think of your business as an energy conversion system. For example:

Money is really just a form of stored energy. It's used to make the exchange of products and services (other forms of stored energy) more efficient. But money is just a tool. If one business wanted to trade its pigs for some cows in barter, both the pigs and cows would be similar energy sources too.

Resources include power sources that the organization has available to it, including the stored energy potential of the people, materials, natural resources, know-how, and capital equipment involved. Obviously, every organization needs resources to be successful.

Clout is the influence and good will that the organization has built up over time. Every business needs clout. Great companies nurture and defend the clout of their brand because they know that if they lose it—for example, if consumers lose trust in the brand—then they've lost a critical asset or energy source.

If your company is operating within a growing market opportunity where there's a lot of customer demand (i.e., there are a lot of potential new energy sources in the form of money, resources, and clout) and if it can efficiently meet that demand, then it will be successful. But if the market needs change, then the company must adapt to meet those needs or it will cease to exist too. The secret to business strategy, therefore, is to use your capabilities to find and maintain integration with growing market opportunities so that your business can get plenty of new energy now and in the future.

To see how a successful business efficiently extracts energy from its environment, take a look at the top three U.S. companies by market capitalization on October 7, 2011: Exxon (XOM), Apple (APPL), and Microsoft (MSFT). Notice what they all have in common. Each, in its own way, has successfully created its own "ecosystem" to extract more available energy from the environment than its competitors.

Exxon, for example, owns or controls every aspect of petroleum production. It owns the wells, the pipes, the refineries, the trucks, the ships, the mineral rights, and the retail distribution. It's capable of extracting more dollars, resources, and clout out of the petroleum industry than any other competitor. You may hate Exxon as a company but there's no denying that they are extremely effective and efficient at what they do and their market cap reflects that. Of course, if the environment changes—if all the oil and gas runs out, if new green fuels become practical alternatives, or if the planetary environment changes radically enough from carbon emissions, Exxon will need to adapt or perish. And it must start adapting before it's too late.

Apple is the same way. Notice how with iTunes, iCloud, iPhone, iPad, MacBooks, and its App Store, as well as its other online and retail distribution channels, it easily extracts new energy from its ecosystem. Once you have an iPhone, you're now "locked into" the ecosystem and you conveniently buy apps from the App Store. If you reflect back on just a few years ago, Apple was out of cash and low on hope while Microsoft was the world's dominant company. Of course, Microsoft built its empire in the 1980s around an ecosystem of desktop computers and the software that runs them. And notice, too, how Microsoft ate Apple's lunch for many decades and now Apple is returning the favor. What happened? The environment changed! Apple has managed to powerfully shape and respond to today's environment while Microsoft has not.

Not All Opportunities and Capabilities Are Created Equal

To get new energy from the environment, a business must use its capabilities to find and integrate with opportunities in the environment. For example, a dentist's office has capabilities including teeth cleaning and repair, front office administration, and marketing. In the surrounding environment are opportunities—people who have cavities or who want a whiter smile and healthy gums. If the dentist's office can use its capabilities to attract customers to its practice and produce positive and desired results for them, then those clients will give energy (money) in return. If the dentist is really good, if he or she is able to produce positive and desired results consistently, then it will be easier to get those clients to return and send their friends (more sources of energy). The same holds true for Apple, Microsoft, and Exxon, as well as for a cheetah on the plains of Africa. Success is about aligning capabilities with opportunities.

However, it should be readily apparent that not all opportunities and capabilities are equally valuable. Opportunities exist on a spectrum of growing to shrinking, while capabilities exist on a spectrum of unique to generic.

Opportunity

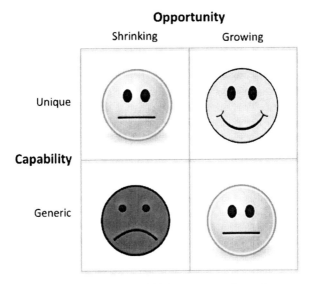

Figure 21. Not all opportunities and capabilities are created equal.

Best: Unique Capabilities with Growing Opportunities

The best strategy is to align unique capabilities with a growing market opportunity (upper right quadrant). If the organization can do this, it will have a very high probability of being successful. Why is this? A growing opportunity means there's a lot of market demand and new energy sources available. At the same time, the organization has developed unique capabilities where there are few real or perceived practical alternatives.

Let's go back to Apple for a moment. As I mentioned before, there's a growing market need for people to be mobile, connect with others, and have access to media and information at their fingertips. There's a big need and thus a big opportunity. Apple has developed capabilities in vision, execution, product design, integrated hardware and software, global supply chain management, marketing, branding, and so on. Because Apple's capabilities are aligned with the current market opportunity (and because there are few practical alternatives to what Apple provides and how well they do it), Apple is incredibly successful right now.

Tolerable: Unique Capabilities with Shrinking Market Opportunities

A less successful strategy is to align unique capabilities with a shrinking market opportunity (upper left quadrant). If you own a market or operate a real or effective monopoly, you can still be successful for as long as the market demand holds. The movie rental chain Blockbuster is a good example. They had unique capabilities in movie aggregation and distribution. Even though people were renting fewer and fewer movies, they were able to hang on and be successful for a time. However, environments can change very quickly, as we saw with the shift from rental tapes and DVDs to online delivery. Even though Blockbuster had a near monopoly in video rental stores, they went bankrupt because the demand shrank so rapidly. Netflix has been better adapted to the new world of online delivery. But notice too how they've gotten a lot of negative publicity for their attempts to serve a dwindling market opportunity (people who still want hard disks in the mail) versus a growing market opportunity (people who want to watch what they want instantly online). Netflix knows, just as Blockbuster knew, that they have to make the leap to serve this new, growing market segment or they'll perish.

Tolerable: Generic Capabilities with Growing Market Opportunities

Another, less effective strategy than the first I mentioned is to serve a growing market opportunity with generic capabilities (lower right quadrant). Just like the last strategy, you can make this work for a time but it's not nearly as fun and lucrative as having unique capabilities in a growing market. For example, imagine a family doctor who runs his or her own practice. Healthcare is a growing market. The doctor has capabilities to diagnose and treat disease. S/he may even be an incredibly talented practitioner with an empathetic bedside manner and a sincere desire to see patients get well. So what? The doctor still struggles to earn a living and pay the bills. Why? Because the market (including customers, vendors, and the insurance industry) views the doctor as just one of thousands of practical alternatives from which to choose.

It's important to point out that it doesn't matter how unique you think your capabilities are. It's how the market perceives your capabilities that matters. If there are a lot of perceived practical alternatives, it's harder to be successful. That's why in crowded industries, the more narrow your focus is, the broader your appeal. Often, the most successful practitioners are those who specialize in one particular discipline: the best brain surgeon for meningioma or the best realtor for high-end homes in 90210. Businesses that successfully differentiate themselves create the perception of unique capabilities. That's why advertising was created. Companies use advertising to try to differentiate themselves from other practical alternatives in the marketplace, calling out what makes them unique and why the market should care. And that's also why the saying "perception creates reality" is so poignant. Because it does.

Terrible: Generic Capabilities with Shrinking Market Opportunities

The least successful strategy by far is to be in a shrinking marketplace with generic capabilities (lower left quadrant). If this is you, then you are suffering and you will continue to suffer. There is an ever-decreasing amount of available energy in the marketplace. There's a free-for-all in the competition, who fight for the scraps, and you must adapt or perish. For example, I knew a lot of real estate agents in Santa Barbara during the boom. The environment changed during the bust. Most of them wisely left the industry and attempted to transition their capabilities (sales, networks, contract negotiations, etc.) into other growing industries where there's greater opportunity. Others who have stuck with it have done so by focusing on a niche: "I'm the foreclosed property specialist" or "I have over 25 years' experience successfully selling Montecito estates. I've been here through booms and busts and I'm you're agent!" But all of these strategies are an attempt to wait out a bad market and be there when—and if—it improves. The environment is king.

The Challenge and the Opportunity

To recap, the goal of any business strategy is to get new energy from the surrounding environment. The obvious challenge to maintaining integration between unique capabilities and growing market opportunities is the fact that the organization, its products and services, and the market conditions are constantly changing. As Darwin made clear, adapting to change can be a life-or-death struggle. It's hard to anticipate change, to understand its ramifications, and to adapt in the right timeframe and sequence. It's challenging to acquire enough resources in capabilities, time, energy, and money to adapt successfully. It's also difficult to prioritize between the immediate needs of today and investing in the future.

Don't underestimate the difficulty of adapting. It is a big challenge indeed. In spite of this, it's possible and it happens all the time. The name of the game in strategy is keeping your organization tightly integrated with growing opportunities. If you can convert that available energy profitably and make it productive, then you'll be very successful. Here's how to do that.

Lex Sisney

Lifecycle Strategy

There is a key insight that makes adapting to change and executing the right strategy more attainable. It's this: All systems evolve in a particular pattern called a *lifecycle*. By learning to recognize the lifecycle stages of your organization, its products, and the market (as well as the different sets of milestones, challenges, and metrics of each), you can correctly adapt your strategy, in the right time and sequence, and improve your probability of success.

A lifecycle simply means that something is born, grows, ages, and ultimately dies. It's easy to spot a lifecycle in action everywhere you look. A person is born, grows, ages, and dies. So does a star, a tree, a bee, or a civilization. So does a company, a product, or a market. Everything has a lifecycle.

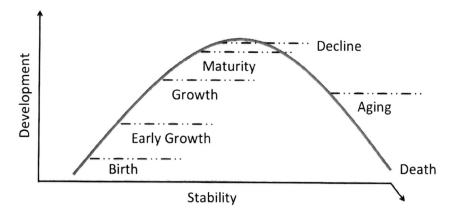

Figure 22. Everything follows a lifecycle.

All lifecycles exist within a dynamic between system development and system stability. When something is born, it's early in its development and it also has low stability. As it grows, both its development and stability increase until it matures. After that, its ability to develop diminishes over time while its stability keeps increasing over time. Finally, it becomes so stable that it ultimately dies and, at that moment, loses all stability.

That's the basics of all lifecycles. We can try to optimize the path or slow the effects of aging, but ultimately every system makes this progression. Of course, not all systems follow a bell curve like the picture above. Some might die a premature death. Others are a flash in the pan. A few live long and prosper. But from insects to stars and everything in

102

between, we can say that everything comes into being, grows, matures, ages, and ultimately fades away. Such is life.

The Three Strategy Lifecycles

What do the principles of adaptation and lifecycles have to do with your business strategy? Everything. Just as a parent wouldn't treat her child the same way if she's three or thirty years old, you must treat your strategy differently depending on the lifecycle stage. And when it comes to your business strategy, there are actually three lifecycles you must manage. They are the product, market, and execution lifecycles. The *product lifecycle* refers to the assets you make available for sale. The *market lifecycle* refers to the type of customers to whom you sell. The *execution lifecycle* refers to your company's ability to execute.

In order to successfully execute on a strategy, the stages of all three lifecycles must be in close alignment with each other. Why is alignment important? Because aligning the product, market, and execution lifecycles gives your business the greatest probability of getting new energy from the environment now and capitalizing on emerging growth opportunities in the future. As you'll see, aligning all three lifecycles also decreases your probability of making major strategic mistakes.

Figure 23 below shows a picture of what alignment among the product, market, and execution lifecycles looks like. This depiction will make more sense after you read the coming chapters that explain each lifecycle and the rationale for aligning them. I'm showing it to you now to give you an intuitive hit of what you're after when it comes to your business strategy. Basically, alignment of all three lifecycles looks like this:

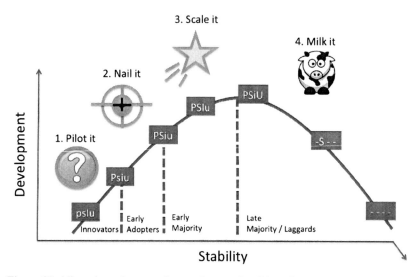

Figure 23. Aligned product, market, and execution lifecycles.

Before I explain each lifecycle in the coming chapters, please note that each stage blends into the next. Although I may speak of distinct stages, this is really only for convenience. There's no real, definitive, clean and clear break where you know when one stage has ended and another has begun.

In addition, there are three basic prerequisites that you must have before you can pursue any strategy. First, the strategy must be aligned with the company vision and values. Second, the company must have or be able to get the resources—including staff, technology, and capital—to execute the strategy. Third, the company must have or be able to develop the core capabilities to execute the strategy. For now, I am going to assume that you have all three prerequisites in place and that you're currently acting on, or about to act on, a strategy that meets these basic requirements.

10. The Product Lifecycle

The "product" is the assets you make available for sale, including products and services. Every product goes through a lifecycle that is a trade-off between product development and product stability. Within the Organizational Physics framework, the basic stages of the product lifecycle are: Pilot It, Nail It, Scale It, Milk It, or at any time, Kill It. Not every product makes it through each stage. Most products get killed before they ever reach the Pilot It stage. However, if a product is to be successful, then it must move sequentially through each stage (there's no skipping) by performing a key set of actions.

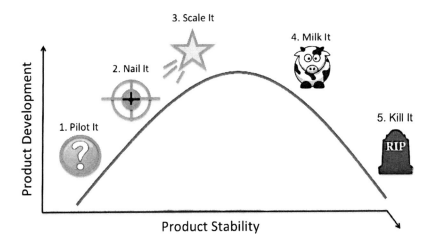

Figure 24. The stages of the product lifecycle.

In the Pilot It stage, the key actions you'll want to take are asking a lot of questions and testing your assumptions. At this stage, you should be seeking to innovate with a product that has the potential to disrupt the status quo. You accomplish this by understanding the real dynamics within a market niche and by creating solutions that solve a market problem in a new and better way. At this stage, you must show thought leadership and be able to articulate why your innovative approach is superior. The ultimate goal at this stage is to have early-stage, innovator-type customers who are enthusiastic champions of your approach.

In the Nail It stage, you focus product development on producing tangible, verifiable results for early adopter clients. At this stage, you sacrifice what's not absolutely essential in the product and relentlessly focus on solving the core customer pain, problem, or need. Your mindset

105

is like a detective's—you're investigating what really works and what doesn't. This requires that you cultivate and collaborate very closely with customer product champions while simultaneously proving and documenting that you have, in fact, solved the market problem. The ideal outcome at this stage is that you've built trust and credibility with early adopter clients and you have paying customers who come back to buy more. Customers buying more—repeat buyers, a contract extension, rolling out to more properties, buying additional units, etc.—provides the only real evidence that you have, in fact, nailed it.

In the Scale It stage—because you've demonstrated thought leadership and proven that you've nailed the product in the prior stages—you're now in a race to be a niche market leader. You must now accomplish two seemingly contradictory things. First, you must stabilize or standardize the product to achieve economies of scale. This allows you to increase your margins because you can now leverage customers' willingness to pay (and because you've proven that you solved their problem at the prior stage, they will be willing to pay). You can also leverage greater internal efficiencies that come from standardizing the product. Once the product is standardized, you must also create high-value add-on products and services. These add-on products could include new line extensions as well as new applications of the core product offering. The ultimate goal at this stage is to increase your product margins while aggressively capturing market share among early majority clients.

In the Milk It phase, your key actions are around maintaining the product for late majority/laggard clients. Now is the time to attempt to leverage your past thought leadership, proven capabilities, and standardization to defend and expand your relative market share. But instead of investing for long-range product development, you limit additional investment to immediate ROI. That is, if required new product investments can't demonstrate an immediate payback, you don't make them at this stage. There's a constant trade-off to be made between continuing to milk the product and selling it off. Of course, at any time the product can be killed because it's no longer viable in the marketplace, it's no longer generating positive ROI, or a buyer cannot be found. The ultimate goal at this stage is to use the cash proceeds, brand position, company resources, and expertise cultivated during the past lifecycle stages to develop new products and services that will, in turn, progress through their own product/market/execution lifecycles.

11. The Market Lifecycle

J ust as every product goes through a lifecycle that is a trade-off between development and stability, so does every market. The market lifecycle is segmented into the types of customers (or potential customers) you're selling to: innovators, early adopters, early majority, and late majority/laggards.

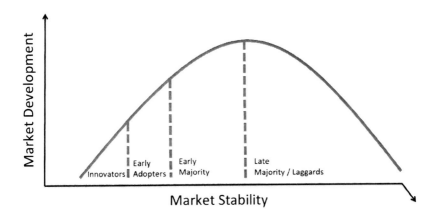

Figure 25. The Market Lifecycle.

The market lifecycle begins with innovators (Pilot It stage). This is the group that drives change within their industry. As technology enthusiasts who tend to be on the lookout for new technologies and new approaches, they are willing to invest time and interest (though usually not money) on vetting them. The key to working with this group is to show thought leadership around why your approach is unique, transformative, and better than the status quo and to be straightforward about what your product can and cannot do. You want to get them excited and invested in your view of the world and your product vision and capabilities. Their endorsement of your approach is essential because it informs the next stage of customers who are not only innovative but also legitimate and worth pursuing.

The next group of customers is the early adopters (Nail It stage). This group is seeking a fundamental breakthrough around a core business problem or strategic opportunity. Because you've shown thought leadership at the prior stage, this group can now start to see how your product can help them achieve their own vision. That is, if your product seems to match their ideas of what could be, then they will be willing to take substantial risks in time and energy, reputation, and money to help make it happen. They are more conceptual than technical. They also find it easy to imagine, understand, and appreciate the benefits of your approach and can relate its potential benefits to their own concerns. This group tends to move and act quickly and they're usually in a big hurry, putting increasing time pressure on your product development schedule.

It doesn't matter that your company is small or unproven when working with early adopters. It only matters that you can produce results and help them achieve their vision. The key to working with this group is collaborating very closely with them to uncover and solve their core problem. This can be challenging because a true early adopter is easy to sell to and very hard to please. They are pursuing their own dream and, consequently, their product demands may be at odds with your own needs to create a universal product with broad market adoption. If you're not careful, you can end up spending too much time and money on unnecessary product features and functions that don't apply to later market stages. If, on the other hand, you can work with select clients within this group to define the core business problem, prove that you solve it, and document this with metrics, testimonials, and case studies, then you are ready to market to the next segment, the early majority.

The early majority segment is known as the practical buyers (Scale It stage). According to Geoffrey A. Moore in his book *Crossing the Chasm*, if a product requires a change in behavior (or a modification of how the early majority customers use other products and services they rely on), then the gap between the needs of the early majority and the prior stage is significant. This gap or "chasm" shows that the psychological profile of the early majority customer is quite different from that of the prior early adopter stage.[8] While the early adopters of the prior stage are willing to take risks and act in isolation, the early majority is much more thoughtful and cautious. They like to make decisions by communicating with others and require a complete product that has demonstrated and proven results before they act. For example, while the early adopter would purchase a product that could deliver an 80 percent solution (seeing it as only 20 percent more to go), the early majority would only buy it when it's 100 percent complete. The key to capturing the early majority market is to leverage the proof of performance from the prior stage and to standardize the product so that it is reliable, stable, complete, and easy to use.

Early majority buyers don't like risk, which they view as a potential waste of time and money. They require stability and are extremely loyal

---

[8] Geoffrey A. Moore, *Crossing the Chasm: Marketing and Selling High-Tech Products to Mainstream Customers* (New York: HarperCollins Publishers, 2002).

once won over. Because they spend a good amount of time communicating with others within their own market, they also help to standardize your product across the industry. While the prior stage is driven by the need to achieve a vision or find a breakthrough solution, this stage is all about making sure things are done properly and that the buyer's own reputation is not put at risk. They will focus on the quality of the product, the infrastructure to support the product, and the reliability of service. They'll even want to ensure that you have competition in the marketplace so they can verify that they're purchasing from a proven market leader. They are price-sensitive in that, in the absence of any special differentiation, they will take the good deal.

Finally, the last stage is the late majority/laggards. This group is resistant to new products until they have become the industry norm. They wait until something has become an established standard and tend to buy from large, well-established companies. They purchase only when products are extremely mature, competition in the marketplace is driving low prices, and the products themselves can be treated as commodities. Basically, they like to buy preassembled packages, with everything bundled, at a heavily discounted price. The key to selling to this segment is to be the established leader in the space, to have economies of scale, and to dominate the major distribution channels.

12. The Execution Lifecycle

L
ike the other lifecycles, the execution lifecycle exists within a dynamic between stability and development. The basic stages of the execution lifecycle are birth, early growth, growth, and maturity and from there things descend into decline, aging, and death.

The focus within the execution lifecycle should be to have the right mix of organizational development and stability to support the stages of the product and market lifecycles. That is, the lifecycle stage of the surrounding organization should generally match the lifecycle stage of the products and markets. If it's a startup, the surrounding organization is the entire company. If it's a Fortune 500 company, this includes the business unit that is responsible for the success of the product as well as any aspects of the parent organization that influence, help, or hinder the success of the product.

Figure 26. The stages of the execution lifecycle.

The surrounding organization should act a certain way at each stage of the product/market lifecycle, as you'll see below. Note that, when a force is or should be dominant, it will be referenced with a capital letter:

> When piloting the product for innovators, the company should be in birth mode and be highly innovative and future-oriented (psIu).

> When nailing the product for early adopters, the company should be in early growth mode and be producing verifiable results for its customers (Psiu).

When beginning to scale the product for the early majority, the product and processes should be standardized and streamlined for efficiency (PSiu).

When fully scaling the product for the early majority, the company's internal efficiencies should be harnessed, as well as the capability to launch new innovations and avoid the commodity trap (PSIu).

When milking the product for the late majority/laggards, the company should use the proceeds from the cash cows to launch new products into new markets that will, in turn, progress through their own PSIU lifecycle stages.

It should intuitively make sense that an organization should align its internal environment to closely match the product and market fit. The reality is that most companies fail to do this.

For example, imagine an entrepreneurial startup that has one nascent product and attempts to launch a new one at the same time. Like a teen pregnancy, it's way too soon to be having offspring. The teen isn't mature, stable, or capable enough of raising babies on her own. Similarly, the startup needs to reach scalable growth mode (where there's standardization, positive cash flow, and strong capabilities) before it attempts to launch new business units.

But just as a teen pregnancy is bad, having kids as a geriatric patient is unwise too. For instance, imagine an aging company with a large cash hoard that acquires a smaller, growth-oriented business. Because the acquirer is so aging, heavy, and stable, it smothers the entrepreneurial zeal and doesn't allow the new acquisition to flourish. The same thing occurs when an aging company attempts its own in-house intrapreneurship but doesn't allow the new business unit the freedom and flexibility it needs early in its development. Perhaps it forces the new unit to follow existing company procedures or to work within the existing business infrastructure. All of these demands create an environment that is too stable, heavy, and bureaucratic, making it unlikely that a new company will thrive.

Figure 27. The goal of the execution lifecycle is perpetual renewal.

Of course, the execution lifecycle does not usually look like a neat bell curve. Most new organizations never make it past the first few stages before falling off the curve into a premature death. That is, even though they're young in months, new startups will run into trouble by acting "old" and soon die. Other businesses spend years, even decades, trying to escape one stage of the lifecycle without making the leap to the next stage. Some businesses shoot up the curve really quickly, only to come down just as quickly.

The ultimate goal of the execution lifecycle is to get the business to a strong level of growth and maturity and, before it gets too "old," launch new business units that, in turn, grow into their own states of maturity and have their own offspring. If done correctly, the business can keep renewing itself as market conditions change and be productive for a long, long time. Let's explore in greater detail how to do that.

The Stages of the Execution Lifecycle

The Execution Lifecycle is where the rubber meets the road. It is the most challenging of the lifecycles to evolve through and it controls and influences every other aspect of your strategy. By being aware of the healthy and unhealthy signs at each stage of the execution lifecycle, you can diagnose when your organization is showing unhealthy symptoms, attempt to restore it to health, and improve your chances of navigating the execution lifecycle more smoothly. You can also more astutely diagnose if the organization has the wrong set of forces for a given lifecycle stage and know what forces it needs more (or less) of to get back on track. Finally, you can use the PSIU forces on the execution lifecycle like a roadmap to better anticipate what's ahead.

Within that context, let's create a snapshot of each stage of the execution lifecycle and understand the healthy and unhealthy signs at each stage.

Birth (psIu)

When piloting the product to innovators, the organization should be in birth mode and be highly innovative and future-oriented. Naturally, you need a very innovative organizational culture to bring forward new innovations into the world. You can tell if there's high innovation in the venture if the product idea is disruptive and if the entrepreneur or founding team shows a tremendous amount of enthusiasm for it. Usually, at this stage there is a lot of excited dialogue about the future potential of the business. Often, from the entrepreneur's perspective, the path ahead seems relatively easy, fast, and straightforward. But it never is. It always takes longer, costs more, and presents more twists and turns along the way, than the entrepreneur can even envision at this stage (if they could envision it, they probably wouldn't do it). If the innovative force isn't high at this stage, there's a problem. This is usually an indication that a burning drive, passion, and commitment to the venture are lacking. Without that commitment, the venture will never come fully into being.

The birth mode will last for as long as it's necessary to uncover the key innovations, establish the basis for thought leadership, and get a real sense of the true product/market fit. This could be as little as a few weeks or months for a venture with a well-defined product/market fit up front. Alternatively, if it's the long-range research and development unit of a larger company, it could last indefinitely (i.e., until its financing is taken away). Regardless of how long the birth mode lasts, the organization at this stage of the lifecycle needs to allow for a tremendous amount of flexibility and responsiveness. Think fast, light, flexible, and creative versus slow, heavy, standardized, and process-oriented.

Because the venture needs capital, it should be very cost-conscious in its investments. When it comes to the amount of capital it needs, the organization should be consciously given very little or "just enough" at this stage. Everyone on the team should be wearing multiple hats and there should be just enough capital to be creative, adaptive, and effective at piloting the product, adjusting it, and entering the next stage of the lifecycle. One of the worst things that can befall a new venture is to have access to too much capital too soon. Having too much capital causes the organization to step into strategic follies such as presupposing demand, ramping up for scale too early, becoming arrogant or lazy, or making large investments before things have been tested and proven. Keeping the capital consciously constrained forces the startup to be creative, agile, and adaptive—just what's required at this stage.

The culture of the organization in the birth stage should be open, egalitarian, and transparent but with a strong founder or co-founder who seems to possess the product and market vision in their DNA. This person's innate sense of what the market really needs and what's required in the product is essential to the venture's success. If I've learned one thing in my experience as an entrepreneur and as a coach to others, it's that the right entrepreneur for a new venture has a very clear early sense of what the product and market fit really is. In fact, they see the vision so clearly that they know when to say "yes" to feature ideas and when to say "no" without getting sidetracked by others' opinions. They have an incredibly hyper-developed sense of innovation for this particular market at this point in time. It's almost like having second sight. Consequently, because they see things others can't yet, they should act like a benevolent dictator who is shepherding a new product vision into the world. They're benevolent because it's not about their ego; it's about the mission. It's about the product and the customers and taking a courageous stand to do things in a different or better way. They're a dictator because they sense the solution in their blood. Yes, it's important to gather customer feedback and track and respond to customer data at this stage, but it's even more important that the founder make the strongest attempt possible to find an existing market for the original product idea.

The birth organization shouldn't have highly designed systems, procedures, or other Stabilizing forces. If it's forced to fit into existing systems and procedures too early, this will dampen its ability to be innovative and design the right solution for this new market and product. It shouldn't be investing in new systems and procedures at this stage either because the product/market fit hasn't been verified yet. Those investments need to happen later in the lifecycle. For now, things need to be kept as light and adaptable as possible. At the same time, the company should be planning what it will measure, how it will measure it, and how it will efficiently sell, service, and collect from customers in the coming stage.

To summarize the birth stage: If enthusiasm is waning, if the team is suffering from high entropy, or if the organization can't find the product/market fit before the money runs out or the market window closes, the organization will die a premature death. The company should have a highly innovative leader who seems to know the product/market fit in their DNA. Systems, procedures, and overhead are kept to a minimum. All investments go towards product prototype development and keeping the organization afloat. If the company can navigate this early stage, maintain enthusiasm and desire, keep entropy within the team in check, successfully pilot the product for innovators, and establish its thought leadership, then it can graduate to the next phase of the lifecycle: early growth.

Early Growth (Psiu)

When nailing the product for early adopters, the surrounding organization should be in early growth mode, ruthlessly focused on producing verifiable results for its customers. You can tell if the company has entered early growth mode because the focus has shifted from "Wouldn't it be great if the product did this cool thing?" in the prior stage to "We've got to get the product right and make sales now!" What happens in early growth mode is this: The founding team has made a great commitment in the prior stage, has taken risks, has established a prototype, and must now quickly create adoption for the product. If they can't, the business will run out of money and/or time and it will fail.

This pressure naturally shifts the focus of the organization from what could be (Innovating mode) to what needs to be done now (Producing mode). Both business and product development at this stage should be moving very, very quickly. Early adopter clients pressure the business to get the product completed even faster. There never seem to be enough time, money, and staff to complete all the work that needs to be done. If there's not relentless focus on producing results for early adopter clients at this stage, it's a sign that the organization is off track and is likely pursuing too many opportunities at once or is confused or doubtful about its chosen strategy.

As I mentioned before, the real indicator that a business has nailed the product is that clients pay and then come back and buy more. "More" could mean a continuation of the contract, additional purchases, or increased usage. It's important, however, not to confuse orders with payments. That is, a client saying they want it and will pay for it is not the same thing as collecting the cash. It's easy for a customer to place an order and then delay payment and acceptance terms. So make sure to collect the cash in order to truly verify demand and that the product is producing desired and expected results.

Sometimes a business will choose to forgo revenue at this stage and, instead, focus on user acquisition. Facebook, for example, didn't sell advertising at this stage of its lifecycle and chose to focus on user acquisition first. But you'll notice that the principle is the same: Facebook users give money equivalents (e.g., their time and personal data) to use the service. By focusing first on meeting the needs of its users and growing its user base and usage, the company could choose to defer revenue until the next phase of the lifecycle. During the early growth stage, every business needs to get customers to pay and then get them to pay more (you can replace "pay" with "use" for an advertising-supported model).

The company culture at this stage should be all about finding the right market fit for the current product. Overhead is light. Execution is fast. The entrepreneur must shift from being a benevolent dictator with a powerful vision to a nosy detective who's seeking to confirm what s/he already senses to be true. This is a tricky transition. Good entrepreneurs are able to collect and analyze the data, ask probing questions of the clients and prospects, and quickly piece together multiple pieces of information into a coherent whole. If a market fit can't be found for the current product or if a bigger but different opportunity presents itself, then the company must assess if it should pivot its strategy or stay the course. What makes this especially tricky is that a highly innovative entrepreneur can tend to change course too often or too early when what's really required is just to press on a bit further on the current path. Alternatively, the entrepreneur can be religiously stubborn and, despite all the evidence to the contrary, press on the current path even if it's a bad one. There's a lot to be said for pure gut instinct backed by good data to navigate this stage.

Whatever the strategy, it requires that the company be ruthlessly focused on selling and servicing customers. The company leaders must be deeply intimate with early adopter clients. They must know them, understand them, and be champions in order to see those customers succeed with the product and solve their core business problem. This usually requires that the business go above and beyond the normal call of duty to service the early adopters' needs. This is because, if the product is new, the early adopter clients won't fully understand how to use it to its full potential yet. Neither will the business. Therefore, both the business and the client must collaborate very, very closely and the business needs to do everything in its power to verify the real value of the product. For example, if the product requires the early adopter clients to restructure their own business and hire and train new staff, the business might actually do the work for the client at this stage—just to show that it can be done, how it should be done, and the real benefit of doing it. Once the evidence is gathered, then the business can extract itself and the client can fully step in. Or, the business can charge for the service if that is needed and desired for its overall growth strategy.

Notice this discrepancy: The business must give a great deal of attention and support to its early adopter clients and, at the same time, it hasn't invested in its stabilizing functions—things like infrastructure, systems, staff, or procedures to do so efficiently. Consequently, the business should only focus on meeting the needs of a few early adopter clients—just enough to verify and validate that the product does, in fact, produce desired and positive results for its customers and to give credibility to the next stage of customers. If the business is getting slammed with a lot of customer demand already, then it should make a conscious decision to say "not yet" to those customers who don't fit the early adopter profile. Granted, it can be very hard for an early growth business to recognize when to say "not yet" and who to say it to. Customers may be clamoring for the product, throwing money at the business, threatening to go to the competition, and generally creating a feeding frenzy. How can a business possibly say "no, not yet" to all of that perceived demand?

The only way a business can say "not yet" is to recognize that it can't realistically meet the demands of all those customers anyway. If it does take on all clients, then it will create poor results for them. Selling something that you can't truly deliver creates a series of disasters. It doesn't help to nail the product and verify and document that the product produces awesome results. Instead, when the business has dissatisfied clients, this creates the opposite perception and negative word of mouth spreads quickly. You should also keep in mind that creating a sense of exclusivity is often the best way to sell something. Saying "not yet" allows the business to create a waitlist, accept pre-orders, and get a better sense of future demand.

The reason a business can't service the needs of all their clients yet is that it hasn't made the necessary investments in its stabilizing functions—things like infrastructure, systems, staff, and procedures to sell and service efficiently. These stabilizing functions begin to take shape in the next stage of the lifecycle. But why not have them in place now before nailing the product? Because that's a strategic folly. When a business invests heavily in infrastructure, staff, and systems before nailing the product, it presupposes demand and wrongly assumes an accurate product/market fit. This puts a tremendous overhead burden on the business and makes it much more difficult, costly, and time-consuming to adapt the product to the real market fit. It's like building a foundation before the house is designed. It's much better to have the problem of overwhelming demand without the ability to meet it than it is to have a great ability to meet no demand. You can navigate the business through the former, not the latter. Just remember: First nail it, then scale it.

The business will need an external funding source at this stage and investments should be made in product development and selling, servicing, and documenting a nailed product solution for those few early adopter clients. The company should still be very cost-conscious at this stage. Creative, roll-up-your-sleeves, out-of-the-box solutions to win business, create demand, and find the right product/market fit are born of necessity. Investments in systems, staff, procedures, marketing, PR, and other elements of scaling should be postponed until there's evidence that the product/market fit is right. However, planning and anticipating what's required to standardize and scale the business in the following stage should be happening now. That is, always be thinking and planning one or two steps ahead.

To summarize the early growth stage: The raw enthusiasm should be down slightly from the prior stage because the real work and effort has set in. But commitment to the venture should still be incredibly high. The company should be ruthlessly focused on winning a few key sales and working very closely with those clients to uncover their real spending priorities and to prove and document that their solution is the right one. This evidence will be crucial to scale the business in the coming stages. If the client buys, is satisfied, and then orders more, it's a sure sign that the product is nailed. The business will need to make a concurrent assessment if that's the market they really want to be operating in. If the team is not focused on selling and servicing a few early adopter clients, it's a sign that they are putting the cart before the horse. Overhead should be light and speed should be fast. Most investments should go to product development and providing an unreasonably high level of support to those early clients. If the product is nailed and market demand is validated, then it's on to the next stage of the lifecycle.

Growth (PSiu)

Because the company has been successful in the prior stage, it has satisfied early adopter clients and it has cash flow (or cash equivalents) from operations. When the company is ready to scale the product for the early majority, it must also begin to stabilize its product, sales, support, and operations. This requires the Stabilizing force to increase to complement the Producing force and bring stability, standards, and scalable efficiencies into the business (PSiu). What does the Stabilizing force look like? It's a combination of a new type of hire—individuals with a healthy S in their style—and the development of systems and procedures that make the business more efficient and capable of meeting large-scale demand. If the business can't develop its Stabilizing force, then it won't be able to scale.

You can tell the company is ready to scale because demand for the company's product is increasing in the marketplace. In fact, it should feel like the product is being pulled forward by market demand, rather than having to push demand into the market. This occurs because of the positive experience and proven and documented results of the early adopter clients in the prior stage. Because early majority clients tend to seek references from the early adopters (e.g., "How does ACME perform really?") and from their own peers, having nailed the product in the prior stage is essential. But now the business must meet a new type of demand—the demand of the early majority who expect high quality, high service, good design, and that the product do everything that has been advertised. This obviously requires standards, systems, and procedures to meet this demand efficiently.

The surrounding organizational culture at this stage of the lifecycle needs to shift from detective mode to operator mode. For example, if there was a single salesperson in the prior stage, then the company needs to invest in creating a repeatable sales process and hire more salespeople. If the founder performed marketing as a lone wolf in the last stage, then a formal brand identity and marketing communications system needs to be created and marketing staff hired. If the VP of engineering performed product management and engineering management at the same time, then s/he must choose one of these roles while a dedicated person is hired for the other. If the co-founder in technology operations doesn't have the experience, desire, or talent runway to scale those operations, then s/he must be replaced in that role. Essentially, all that has been run and operated as a light and nimble but chaotic organization where people wear multiple hats must now shift to a more standardized, structured, and disciplined approach to business development.

As the Stabilizing force comes on, the Producing force must continue to drive the business forward. The company should no longer be pinching pennies. Instead, it needs lots of external financing to invest in infrastructure, systems, staff, sales, and outbound marketing so that it can capture the opportunity. And now is exactly the time to invest heavily. If venture capital is required, then just know that smart venture capitalists trip over themselves to get involved with a company that has successfully nailed a product, has repeat sales and/or usage, is showing tremendous thought leadership, has verified a large and untapped market, has low overhead, and has a focused, talented team. Because there's enough Stabilizing force being developed now within the organization, investment capital can be put to good use. Sales can scale. So can marketing, customer service, and product development. Raising capital from the right strategic investors is easy for a company like this. If venture capital isn't required because the company has another external funding source, then that simply enables the company to maintain more of its equity. Either way, the company is well positioned to begin to scale and can soon drive positive cash flow from its prior product investments.

It's critical to make a distinction between "stabilizing the Producing force" and just stabilizing. The Producing force (i.e., producing positive and desired results for customers) is the most important force in any business. The only real purpose of stabilizing is to make the Producing force more efficient and to ensure that the business is controlling for systemic risk (the kind that can destroy the business, such as a lawsuit, theft, or brand damage). With greater efficiencies, the business can produce more results for more clients more profitably. With proper systemic control, the business can help to avoid a calamity. A business must be very mindful, however, that the Stabilizing force not take on a life of its own and run amok with too much heaviness, bureaucracy, or overhead. There needs to be just the right amount of stabilizing so that the company can produce results efficiently for its customers now and in the future and is reasonably well protected from systemic risk.

Navigating this stage of the lifecycle is a very hard transition for an entrepreneur and a business to make. It begins with the people. By nature, most entrepreneurs and early stage employees demonstrate incredibly high Producing and Innovating forces. Naturally, this is what's required to bring a new venture to life. It needs to be organic, adaptable, creative, fast, and ever pushing the needle forward. But now the business must develop its Stabilizing force and this requires the involvement of new people who also naturally have a bigger S in their styles such as pSiu, PSiu, pSIu, or pSiU. There is also a requirement to have much more of a stabilizing focus across all areas of the business. Managing a business at this stage is kind of like parenting a teenager. The parent wants the teen to be well adjusted, get good grades, and find their purpose and calling. But the teen just wants to run wild and party with their friends. If the parent clamps down too hard, the teen will rebel. If they don't clamp down hard enough, the teen will live a wasted youth. Every parent must weigh this inherent conflict and attempt to find the right balance and approach. The same is true for every manager at this stage of the execution lifecycle.

One of two things usually befalls a business at this stage that can cause it to fall off the execution lifecycle curve, experience high entropy, and fail. The first is that the entrepreneur is unable to structure, stabilize, and scale the business and s/he has become a bottleneck to growth. In the past, the entrepreneur has worn multiple hats during the company's development but now things are too big and too unwieldy for a one-man show to manage. The right new people need to be hired, in the right sequence, and for the right roles. Most new entrepreneurs make some mission-critical mistakes in this transition. They either hire the wrong people, place them in the wrong positions, give up too much control, don't give up enough control, or generally get frustrated with how their business is performing and their changing role in the company. It's like a kind of purgatory. If this transition stage has gone on for long enough, the entrepreneur may want nothing to do with the business altogether. In fact, they may be totally burned out and rue the day they ever started it. This decrease in entrepreneurial zeal at this stage is a critical loss because the Innovating force still mostly resides within the founder(s) and hasn't been effectively cascaded into other parts of the organization yet.

The other scenario occurs when venture capitalists or other significant shareholders no longer want the entrepreneur involved with the business—either because s/he has been too slow to scale or has made too many critical mistakes, or because the board feels they're not the right CEO to take the business forward. If the VCs have control, they'll force the founder(s) out and insert their chosen hired gun. While the hired gun may, in fact, be able to bring stability to the business, increase cash flow, and execute a sale (PSiu functions) in the short run, losing the entrepreneur at this stage usually means that the business won't reach its full potential because it also loses its core innovation capability. If the VCs don't have control, it will be a testy and often toxic marriage of necessity until they can sell their stake or get control and oust the founder(s). Both cases cause the organization to suffer from a high amount of entropy and make it less successful than it could be.

There is a right and a wrong way to navigate this transition from startup to professionally managed company. The wrong way is to lose the entrepreneurial zeal of the early founder(s). If this occurs, it's like losing the "heart" of the company. No organization can be truly successful without this. If you look at most of the great businesses in history, the founders are involved through and beyond this stage of the lifecycle. It is their innovation and vision that allows the business to keep adapting and finding new ways to meet customer needs. True entrepreneurial vision and passion isn't something that can just be hired out. For example, if you look at Silicon Valley, you'll notice that the most successful businesses tend to be those with the founders still actively involved in a leadership position. Google. Oracle. Salesforce. Facebook. Apple. If you look beyond that to the most iconic brands of the 20th century, you'll see that the founder played an instrumental role in the company's evolution into maturity and for many years after. IBM. Kodak. Porsche. Toyota. Estée Lauder. Microsoft. Hewlett-Packard. So keeping the founding heart beating for as long as possible is essential to capturing the full opportunity. At the same time, it's wrong for the business to keep acting the way it always has. It's no longer a startup. It must evolve and the founder(s) must evolve too.

The right way to navigate the transition is to create an environment where the founder(s) can embrace more stabilization. This means that they and the rest of the leadership team know who to hire; when to hire them; and what, how, and when to delegate. At the same time, the founder(s) can remain engaged, passionate, and committed to the opportunity so that the innovative capability is put to best use. If the business can get this mix right, then it will navigate beyond growth into maturity with its heart still intact. It has a real chance at lasting success. But if it can't get it right, then it will start to succumb to internal entropy, fall off the lifecycle curve, begin to age prematurely, and ultimately fail.

Now more than ever, it's important to ensure that some key elements of the business are aligned to make the transition from startup to profitable, professionally managed company. They are: (1) aligned vision and values; (2) aligned organizational design or structure; (3) aligned processes or systems; and (4) aligned people. I'll discuss each of these in detail in Part IV.

Up until now, the business systems and processes should have been very light and organic. Now, as the business starts to scale, it will need more robust systems and processes that support the business strategy. There's the need for processes in sales, customer service, accounting, finance, human resources, marketing, product development, strategy, etc. This is obvious. However, many businesses fail in this part of their development because they implement systems that are too cumbersome, hard to manage, and expensive or that are simply misaligned with a changing strategy. The systems should work for the business; the business should not have to work for the systems.

To summarize the growth mode, the company needs to stabilize how it sells and services customers and develops its product. This requires the company to hire a new style of manager, one with more stabilizing characteristics, and to focus on standardizing and systematizing all aspects of business operations. The new hires, who display different and more "professional" ways of doing things, and the high amount of change in how the business operates can be upsetting to old hands. The transition must be accomplished without losing the entrepreneurial heart or staying stuck in the past way of doing things. If a company can do this, then it will be able to operate efficiently and drive growing revenues and profits from its operations. This stage of the lifecycle requires a lot of investment in infrastructure, staff, systems, and procedures. It also calls for increasing investments in outbound sales and marketing efforts. Growth mode is a very challenging transition to make and, to do it well, the company must have aligned vision and values, structure, systems, and people. If navigated correctly, there will be a collective sense within the business that the company is in the right place at the right time and that the sky is the limit.

Maturity (PSIu)

In the prior lifecycle stages, the company has piloted the product for innovators and established thought leadership. Then it nailed the product for early adopters, drove repeat sales, and began to systematize how it operates. Now the company is in full-on scale mode for the early majority customers. It is producing results efficiently and driving revenues and profits. During the prior growth stages, the Innovating force needed to back off so that the company could efficiently produce results in its core product offering without unnecessary or untimely distractions. But now that it's mature, it's time once again to amp up the Innovating force. This means efficiently producing results for clients while simultaneously driving forward new product innovations that extend the life and margins of the product. The company has a healthy combination of stability and development. It's increasing sales, profits, market share, and brand awareness. It's like business nirvana.

However, the instant an organization reaches maturity, it also begins its decline and heads towards aging and, ultimately, death. Why does this occur? Because the organization's stability continues to increase while its development begins to wane (this is what causes the top of the curve in any lifecycle). So, unlike the product and market lifecycles that plan for obsolescence, the goal of the execution lifecycle is one of constant renewal. The real objective is to first move up through birth to early growth, growth, and maturity and, once the organization is at a reasonable level of maturity (but before it begins an irreversible decline), to launch new organizations or business units that successfully develop new products for new markets and progress through their own lifecycle stages. Like a species that produces offspring, launching new business units allows a company to be vibrant, useful, and well adapted to its environment over an extended period of time.

Launching new business units successfully requires that the business have sound alignment in vision and values, structure, process, and people. It must be able to plan, adapt, measure, execute, and respond to future changes. It must have positive cash flow from one or more of its core product offerings to fund the development of new products. It must be able to carve out enough space or oxygen for the new business units to uncover new innovations, nail them, scale them, and repeat the process. This isn't easy to do. Great businesses do it really well over long periods of time. I'll discuss the elements of how to do this later. For now, just recognize that maturity is very hard to reach and the minute a business reaches it, unless the company leadership actively manages against it, it starts its decline into aging and death.

Decline (PSiU), Aging (-S-), and Death (----)

As the company matures, it becomes less change-driving and more change-responding and it enters a decline phase. What happens first is that the Unifying force comes on strong and turns in on itself so that employees become more concerned with politicking and promotions than with meeting customer needs. The Stabilizing force continues to grow so that the Innovating force leaves the organization entirely. It has no room to flourish because things are so stable, inward-focused, and heavy that it can't act to shape the environment. The loss of the Innovating force causes the organization to lose integration with its markets and customers, thereby speeding up its decline. The Stabilizing force continues to increase over time and the company continues to age until it finally loses all integration and falls apart completely in death.

Because the product and market lifecycle plan for obsolescence, the company should milk the cash cow products that are sold to late majority/laggard clients and use those proceeds to invest in new business units in a cycle of perpetual renewal. But it's critical to recognize that if a company is aging itself (not just its products but also its execution capabilities) then it won't be able to successfully launch new products. It's on a fast train to obsolescence itself.

It is very common for an aging company past its prime to have a large cash hoard. The cash has been built up over many years of milking one or more core products. In an effort to stimulate growth, the board of directors first authorizes the company to go out and acquire younger companies with promising technology or that are increasing market share. The new acquisitions, however, don't work to reinvigorate the aging company culture. The entrepreneurs of the acquired companies—sick of the politicking, overhead, and heavy bureaucracy of the parent company—cash in their chips and start a new company or become angel investors or VCs themselves. After enough failed acquisitions, the company becomes a turn-around or take-over candidate itself.

It's important to remember that even a small company (e.g., one early in its lifecycle), if unhealthy, can exhibit the same signs of aging and decay as a larger company. That is, a company doesn't automatically get the right to go the long way up the execution lifecycle. It's more common for it to fall off into aging and decay prematurely along the way. But whether a company is large or small, young or old, if it's exhibiting signs of aging, then it must reinvigorate itself. It does this by choosing the right strategy and by aligning its vision and values, structure, processes, and people. Unlike a brand-new startup, an aging company first has to release the entropy that is holding it back. If it can reduce the amount of energy lost to entropy, then it will free up more energy to find and execute on the new integration opportunities. If not, it will remain stuck in a quagmire until it dies.

Keep Climbing the Mountain

Successfully navigating the execution lifecycle is like climbing a mountain that is forever growing. The mountain itself is made up of problems to solve. Why problems? Because entropy is always at work, causing disintegration. Still, the point is not to solve all your problems (this would mean there's no more change and you're fundamentally dead). The point is to be able to always move on to a higher class of problems. You climb the mountain step by step remembering that the higher you go, the better the view.

In the coming chapters, I will share with you the key indicators that will reveal if your product/market/execution lifecycles are misaligned. I will also explain the well-defined path to strategic success—as well as the three strategic follies you must avoid at all costs.

13. Lifecycle Strategy: How to Tell if You're Doing It Right

So far, you've learned that in order to execute on the right strategy, you should aim to align the product, market, and execution lifecycles. Now we'll take a look at the four key indicators that will tell you if you're on the right strategic path. The key indicators, which must be taken into account at each lifecycle stage, are market growth rate, competition, pricing pressure, and net cash flow.

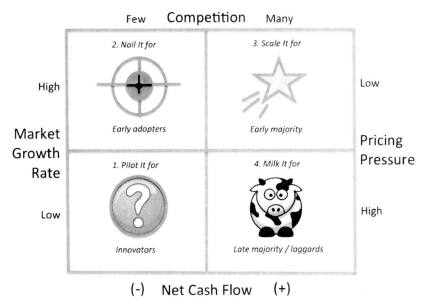

Figure 28. Four key metrics guide the timing and sequence of your strategy: market growth rate, competition, pricing pressure, and net cash flow.

Let's take a visual walk around the figure above and see how the key indicators work. First, notice that when you're piloting your product for innovators in quadrant 1, you should be in negative cash flow. The total invested in the product to date should exceed the return. The market growth rate should be low because you're still defining the problem and the solution for the market. Therefore, the competitors within your defined niche should be few in both number and capabilities. Consequently, the pricing pressure will be high because you haven't defined the problem or the solution, so you have no ability to charge enough money for it at this stage.

As you're demonstrating thought leadership and winning over the innovators, you uncover the real business problem and begin to Nail It for early adopters in quadrant 2. Notice that you're still in negative cash flow at this stage. It is taking considerable investments of time, energy, and money to fund early-stage product development. But as you progress, more and more early adopters jump on board and the market growth rate begins to increase. The competitors should still be few but, because you're proving that you're solving the customer problem, the pricing pressure lessens and you're able to charge more for your product at this stage. That is, you no longer have to give the product away for free or cheap like you did at the prior stage because you're showing that you do, in fact, solve a problem and add value.

As you've nailed the product in quadrant 2, you leap across the chasm into quadrant 3 and begin to scale the product for the early majority by standardizing it. The market growth rate should be high now and increasing. Also, the number of competitors entering the market will be growing because they see the increasing market demand and either think they have a way to do it better or are content to be a "me-too" competitor in a growing pie. Alternatively, they might feel they need to act to defend their existing turf. If you've done the sequence right so far, then you've established thought leadership at the Pilot It stage; you've proven that you've solved the problem at the Nail It stage; and you've standardized the product early in the Scale It stage, which increases your margins. Now is the time to add new high-value extensions and add-on products and services that increase the life and perceived value of the product in the marketplace. This will help you avoid the final product/market stage, the commodity trap in quadrant 4, for as long as possible.

Because you've done the sequence right so far, you should be in a market leadership position and the pricing pressure, even though there's a lot of competition, should still be low for your product in quadrant 3. Just think of how, in spite of many iPhone competitors, Apple still keeps the price of its iPhone high relative to the competition. Others can compete on price but Apple doesn't have to yet—at least not until the market is in a true commodity phase. In this stage, you're finally in positive net cash flow for this product and you've got standards, leadership, and demand. All of your hard work should be paying big dividends.

Quadrant 4 is known as the "commodity trap." Your goal is to avoid this commodity trap for as long as possible by continuing to create high-value product extensions in quadrant 3. But when you ultimately arrive at quadrant 4 (all markets ultimately do), the market growth rate is slow because the fundamental problem has been solved for most customers. For example, if everybody has an iPod, there's no longer a growth market for the product. During the preceding stages, a lot of competition has emerged and they are still attempting to compete, often on price.

Consequently, the pricing pressure is really high. Despite these challenges, if you've done the preceding product/market sequence correctly, you have a cash cow that can print money until it's finally sold or killed off.

Investment Capital: Timing and Sources

One of the greatest concerns for growth oriented companies is when and how to get financing. Financing from external sources is always required to successfully navigate the product through the pilot it and nail it phases and to ramp up for scale. "External" simply refers to sources other than the product itself. For example, when a product is in the Pilot It and Nail It phases, it generates negative net cash flow. It will need additional financing to make it to scale. Often, when a product is in scale mode, it may need more capital sources to fund expansion, staffing, and aggressive sales and marketing. Different types of external financing sources are leveraged at different stages. If this is a new product launch funded within a parent company, then the parent often takes on the burden of funding the new product until it is in scale mode and generating positive net cash flow. It can be helpful to recognize in advance which type of external financing typically participates at each stage of the product/market/execution lifecycles.

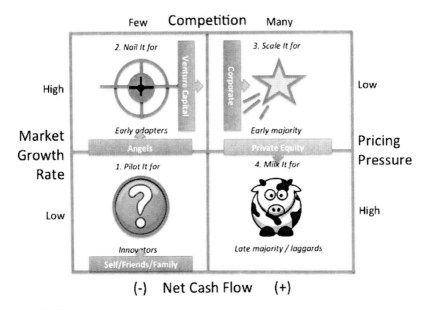

Figure 29. Typical investment capital timing and sources.

Pilot It Stage (Starting in Quadrant 1)

Financing early in the Pilot It stage is usually a combination of self-financing and the contributions of friends and family. The entrepreneur takes out a loan, invests proceeds from a previous venture, or gets friends and family to participate as early investors. Note that friends and family invest because they trust the entrepreneur, not because the business proposition and path to exit are clear at this stage.

Pilot It to Nail It Stage (Moving from Quadrant 1 to 2)

Angel investors usually participate between the Pilot It and Nail It stages. This occurs because a product prototype has been developed (this could be as simple as a PowerPoint or screenshots) and the business case is significantly clearer than at the prior stage. Angel investors are willing to take tremendous risk in exchange for a lower valuation on the company and most will seek to help the company figure out how to really nail the product and ultimately get it ready for scale and future investors.

Nail It to Early Scale It Stage (Moving from Quadrant 2 to 3)

Venture capital investments usually take place between the Nail It and early Scale It stages—once the company has demonstrated that they have nailed the product and understood the market problem and when market demand is clear and the company needs capital to scale. The VC will offer capital and access to resources such as staff, market connections, and expertise to scale the business. Their focus is to invest at a low enough valuation that can generate a significant return on investment later on through a sale of the company or an initial public offering (IPO).

Corporate investors also participate at this stage but for different reasons than VCs. They invest to acquire rights or interest in a promising technology that fits their own strategic roadmap. This type of technology acquisition gets a lower valuation than if the company had scaled itself into a profitable growth mode. Often a smaller company with patented and/or promising technology will seek to sell to a much larger company at this stage so that the founders can create liquidity and the new parent company can leverage its larger sales, distribution, and customer support staff to support the rollout of the acquired technology into scale.

Scale it Stage (Moving across Quadrant 3)

Once the company enters its scale mode and is generating significant cash flow, and if it has a clear opportunity to capture a significant market opportunity, then it will do one of three things to get external financing. One, the company will do an IPO. Two, the company will sell itself to a larger company. In this case, the valuation is usually much higher than the previous technology-only acquisition because the acquirer is buying more than just a technology—it is also buying the future cash flows, profits, and budding brand awareness of the seller. Or three, the company will choose some type of bridge or mezzanine financing that helps to bridge the financing gaps that appear when a company is attempting to scale up but isn't ready for an IPO or strategic sale yet.

Milk it Stage (Moving from Quadrant 3 to 4)

This stage is less about business growth and more about cost cutting, roll-up acquisitions, and financial engineering. Private equity groups use their war chest and access to cheap capital to acquire other companies that can be repackaged for a future sale. Large corporate acquisitions are made as well, but it's usually for the cash flow that the businesses generate or for the existing patents, customers, or distribution channels. How Wall Street reacts to the deal is usually viewed as more important than the fundamental business principles at work. Radical new innovations that are required in the prior stages are viewed as distractions to be avoided in this stage.

The Path to Prosperity: Doing It Right

Understanding how to align the product/market/execution lifecycles reveals the path to strategic success. This path goes the long way around, as depicted in figure 30 below.

Simply put, you will need to pilot your product for innovators first, then nail it for early adopters, and only then scale it for the early majority. If you follow this sequence correctly, then you create maximum building of market awareness; you make smart, timely investments relative to market readiness; you maintain pricing and margins; and you avoid the commodity trap for as long as possible. That's the real path to prosperity for any new business venture.

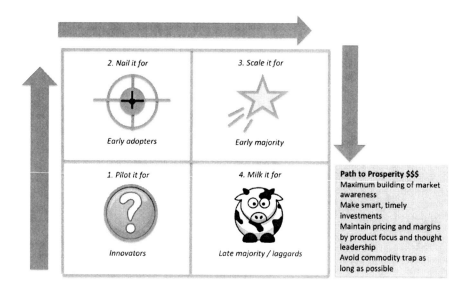

Figure 30. The Path to Prosperity goes the long way around.

Just because success requires taking the long way around doesn't mean that it has to take a long amount of time. As the late John Wooden said, "Be quick, but don't hurry." There's real, hard work to be accomplished. It needs to be completed in the right sequence and there will be many ongoing, necessary adjustments to the strategy. But no matter what, you have to follow the sequence. No skipping, no shortcuts, and no racing ahead before it's time.

The Three Strategic Follies

There are three classic strategic follies that cause companies to fail in their strategy execution. Essentially, all three strategic follies occur when a company attempts to bypass the long way around the product, market, and execution lifecycles and tries to find shortcuts instead. The three strategic follies are the Face Plant, the Flame Out, and the Lost Opportunity.

The Face Plant

The first folly is what I call the Face Plant. This happens when an entrepreneur is innovating on a product but targeting a commodity market. The company foolishly spends resources to solve a problem that the market views as already having been solved. The company doesn't establish thought leadership in quadrant 1 and doesn't nail it and prove that it can solve the underlying problem in quadrant 2. Therefore, it doesn't understand the true customer spending priorities and fails to create a product that meets them. It never establishes profit margins in quadrant 3 and so it comes into a commodity market against better-financed and more robust solutions, quickly getting crushed by those vendors with a more complete service offering.

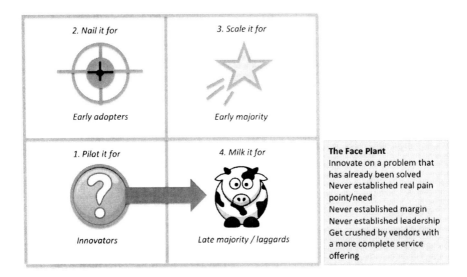

Figure 31. The Face Plant.

It's obvious that you don't want to pilot a product directly into a commodity market. After all, no one in their right mind would invest innovation dollars into land-based telephones today. (Note: Some entrepreneur may, in fact, invest in new land-based phones but they would do so by discovering a disruptive opportunity in the process of going the long way around the strategic path). What happens to many entrepreneurs is that they are so focused on product development and product features, that they don't simultaneously validate and develop a market. They have a product in search of a problem. If the company isn't testing, selling, and validating its early product prototypes with innovators and early adopters, then it runs a high risk of falling directly into a commodity trap.

For example, several years ago I was introduced to a start-up company in New York—we'll call them CompanyX—that was building an online personal financial management tool. The founders were intelligent and passionate. At the time, Quicken Online, Microsoft Money, Mint, and Wesabe were already operating in the space. After the basic introductions and overview, I asked them some basic questions to get a sense for their approach. What struck me was that, although the founders were big believers in the technical features of the product, they hadn't really considered who the target customer was and what core problems still needed to be solved. Instead, they had their heads down building new product features. Their basic assumption was that if they built a great product, consumers would respond and come in droves.

I explained that, even though they believed they were different or unique compared to the competition, having better tools alone wouldn't cut it. At that stage in the product/market lifecycle, the market would view them as just another "me-too" competitor—but one with significantly less brand awareness, consumer trust, and resources. Even though this was a relatively recent, four- or five-year-old market, it was, in effect, a commodity one. Consumers could get any number of free online financial tools that seemed to meet most needs. No clear problem remained unsolved. Unless they could uncover a niche with an unsolved problem—going the long way around the strategic path and uncovering new growth opportunities—there would be little to gain as a me-too competitor with some hard-to-explain technical benefits. They'd never compete. The company continued on its path anyway but was never able to get traction in the market and they shut down operations a short time later.

I share this story because it's very easy for an entrepreneur to become enraptured with why his or her product is unique or different in the marketplace and the reality is . . . that's not what counts. What counts is how the market perceives you and if there's a significant problem or need that you solve. If you're going up head-to-head against a market leader with more capital, brand awareness, and overall traction, you can't compete on improved technical features alone. Nor can you compete on being a low-cost, me-too provider because you've never established your profit margins through standardization and scale. Instead, you'll need to go the long way around and catch or create the next wave of innovation. Like Wayne Gretsky, you don't skate to where the puck is—you skate to where it's going.

What's interesting about this story is that the competitor, Mint.com, which started a few years earlier than CompanyX, did navigate the path to prosperity and achieved great success. By the time I had my meeting with

CompanyX, Mint.com had already successfully piloted their product for innovators and nailed it for early adopters. Shortly after that, they quickly scaled the business by adding over 3,000 users per day. In fact, just a year or so later, Mint.com was sold to Intuit for $170M.

It may seem counter-intuitive to view a relatively new market (one just five years old like the online personal financial space) as a commodity market. The reality is that the Face Plant doesn't have to occur only in an old, legacy market. In fact, as technology cycles continue to shorten and the world becomes increasingly interconnected online, the length of time to navigate a product and market lifecycle will continue to shrink too. This is all the more reason to learn to identify and execute well on new growth opportunities.

The Flame Out

The next strategic folly is what I call the Flame Out. The Flame Out occurs when a company tries to scale prematurely. Usually this happens when the founding team, in a hurry to get cash flow from sales or because they believe the market window is closing, attempts to aggressively ramp up sales without having nailed the product first. Because the company hasn't nailed the product and proven that they've done so, they don't understand the customer's real pain and spending priorities. They make a big marketing push and create a lot of market noise, but this doesn't translate into real adoption and sustainable revenue and profits. In fact, it often results in dissatisfied early majority clients who are upset because the product doesn't do what it promises or what they need and is rife with bugs and errors.

Lex Sisney

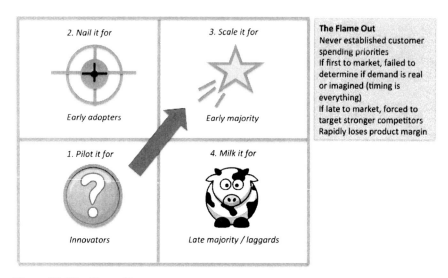

Figure 32. The Flame Out.

In life and in business, timing is everything. So how do you know that you've nailed it and should proceed to the Scale It stage? The only real indicator of having nailed it is that the early adopter clients have purchased the product and they come back to buy or use more. For example, a classic strategic mistake is when a company believes they've nailed it because the product meets the founder's vision or because a lot of companies are expressing early interest in their solution. Then, in the race to get a return on investment and to respond to the apparent demand, they quickly launch into scale mode without truly understanding the customers' pain points or true spending priorities. The company spends enormous sums of money, launches in a big way, and causes a lot of market noise but fails to convert interest into paying, repeat customers. This could be because the market is not ready or the features are not aligned right. Essentially, the company presupposes demand when the demand isn't really there—so the company flames out.

Software as a service (SaaS) firms often make this mistake by confusing customer interest or trial signups with actually nailing it. For example, I was introduced to a company building a mobile application platform for sports stadiums. Without hardly any outbound marketing, the company is receiving a tremendous amount of interest from sports teams and stadiums around the world. There's also a lot of competition emerging. So the time pressure is extremely high to get their product fully built, easy to use, and rolled out at scale to meet this demand before the market window closes.

136

However, what's really essential is that the company first proves that they have solved the core business problem for a few key stadiums—driving on-site revenue and improving the spectator experience. Nailing the product requires the company to put on its detective hat and spend an inordinate amount of time, energy, capital, and attention on really understanding stadium operations, the fan experience, and the core business problem to solve. They'll know they've solved it once usage rates are high and that handful of Nail-It-phase clients is happy, willing to pay because the value has been realized, and clamoring to expand the solution out to the rest of their holdings or to buy more advanced features. The company must document this interest (through case studies, endorsements, metrics, etc.) for the entire world to see.

If they can figure out how to nail it and make it easy to use their product, then more stadiums will readily buy their solution, come back, and buy more. "Install our app, use our methods, and you can expect to increase onsite revenue by 25 percent and create a better fan experience, as shown by these other stadiums like you." With evidence and endorsements like that, how could another prospect stadium refuse? And notice, too, that even if another competitor had scaled earlier with more stadiums in their portfolio, it would be possible to knock that competitor out using better evidence, a proven model, and a better approach developed by really nailing the product.

Once a product is really nailed, it becomes possible to scale. The detective hat shifts to a factory mindset. The company standardizes its learning and is now in the race to achieve dominant market share. The demand from the market should be increasing. In fact, it will feel like the company is being pulled into the market by customer demand, rather than having to create demand through outbound marketing. Remember, early majority clients buy during scale mode and the evidence they use to make purchases is the endorsements and data from early adopters in the Nail It stage. First you've got to nail it; then you can scale it.

Another important factor in nailing it before scaling it is aligning with market timing. In your own investigations and efforts to really solve the core business problem, you may find that the market really isn't ready yet or that a critical piece of underlying technology hasn't matured enough. You may find a host of other indicators that tell you to dial down or dial up your expansion plans. Don't be the company that does a global launch based on a vision of the future that doesn't exist yet. To avoid the Flame Out, spend the time and invest the resources to nail the product and validate product and market fit first.

That said, there is a risk of spending too much time nailing the product rather than scaling it. This risk shows up when a company is

Lex Sisney

spending too much time and capital designing the ideal product with every feature and function under the sun for its early adopter clients. Or else it's designing a product for the wrong type of customer for this stage of the lifecycle. Instead, the company must only prove that it solves the core customer problem with its minimal viable product. Then it can focus its efforts on developing features and functions that meet the needs of the next customer stage, the early majority, through standardization and scale.

The Lost Opportunity

The third strategic folly is what I call the Lost Opportunity. In this stage, a company pilots it for innovators and nails it for early adopters but can't execute quickly or efficiently enough to get to scale. The market window closes because some other company executes more quickly or efficiently, nails it, then scales it, captures the leadership position, and reaps the benefits. The lost opportunity company then tries to compete on price and pushes the product into the market as if it were a commodity. But because they haven't standardized their product and established market leadership, the product hasn't created the brand awareness and margins to be successful. It's like a fruit that dies on the vine.

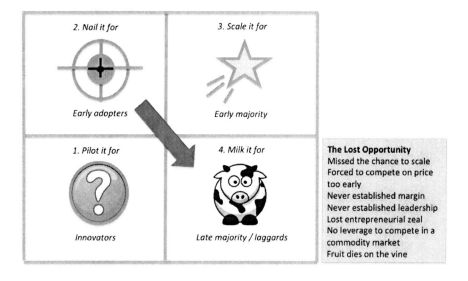

Figure 33. The Lost Opportunity.

For me, this is the saddest strategic folly. All entrepreneurs are in it for the opportunity. Entrepreneurs absolutely hate to miss an opportunity, especially one into which they invested so much passion, sweat, and tears. It's gut-wrenching to recognize that the business will never really make it to scale and some form of lucrative success. Sure, it may turn out to be a nice lifestyle business but you'll always be playing a distant third or fourth to the market leaders. And that's not a game that entrepreneurs truly want to play.

What usually happens in this scenario is that the entrepreneur eventually loses their passion for the opportunity. If the business is operational and backed by investors, then the entrepreneur gets fired or kicked out and a professional manager attempts to find an exit, usually by selling to a larger competitor for a bargain price. If the business is operational but the founders still have control, they'll continue to operate the business in the hopes of selling it one day but their entrepreneurial fire will be gone. The business will be a former shell of itself and its once promising potential. The opportunity is lost even if no one openly admits it.

The right course of action when dealing with a lost opportunity is to admit it. You're too late. You'll never be one of the market leaders in that particular space, nor will you have the margins, cash flow, and terrific success you're seeking. It's time to gather your resources and find a new opportunity (based on past learning and insights) and pivot into a new strategy that you can leverage into a scalable growth phase.

When you speak with most successful entrepreneurs, you'll learn that they've had their share of failed business ideas, often because some other company beat them to the punch. Rather than continuing on that path or giving up, they eventually pivot their original idea into a new market opportunity or make an adjustment to the product that serves an untapped opportunity—and that's what ultimately makes them successful.

I started my first company in Minnesota in 1996, when I was 26 years old. My vision was to provide an electronic procurement service for small- and mid-size companies using corporate intranets. This was back in the day when the term "intranet" was just being coined. I moved back home to my mom's llama ranch in rural Minnesota and, with a website, a business plan, and a cell phone, began to live my dream. Or so I thought. After a year of effort and spending all my personal savings, I was feeling really dejected because I had little to show for my efforts. I had no customers, no real product, no team, and no capital. Besides, I was beginning to hear rumors of two companies on the west coast that were operating in the same space, Ariba and CommerceOne. In March, when Minnesota is dreary, brown, and muddy, I flew out to meet with Ariba in Menlo Park, California, and see what was what.

I remember a few things about that trip. First, it was a classic sunny, beautiful day in California. As I parked my rental car in front of their offices, my mouth fell open. While I was working out of a small bedroom, here was a beautiful, modern office building jam-packed with people and buzzing with activity. The phones were ringing off the hook, there was energy and excitement, they had raised a bunch of venture capital, and they had hired an experienced management team. They were scaling out their sales force and had large Fortune 100 clients coming on board. I was absolutely crushed. There was no way I was going to compete with these guys. The opportunity was clearly lost!

I sulked around for a few months trying to figure out what I was going to do next. I moved out of my mom's place and into the city. I started dating again (hey, entrepreneurship is all-consuming) and took odd jobs to pay the rent and plan my next steps. One morning, I read an article in *The Wall Street Journal* about a new marketing program created by Amazon.com. It was ingenious. Rather than paying up front for its ads, Amazon was offering a commission to anyone who sent them an online visitor who bought something. "Imagine that," I thought, "only pay for your advertising if it results in a sale!"

I started to look more closely at the space and play around with different solutions. Even though there were two much larger competitors in the market already, I felt that there was still a big, unsolved problem and that I could solve it using the same methods I created for the electronic procurement business I had just closed down. I went back to the angel investors who didn't invest in my last venture, pitched them again on the new opportunity, and I was in business! That new company, born out of the ashes of the old one, went on to become the industry leader in its space, generating hundreds of millions of dollars in sales. Most clichés are true, including this one: "When one door shuts, another one opens." If you find yourself in a Lost Opportunity and the passion is still there, keep looking for the next open door.

Remember: Go the Long Way Around!

The path to strategic success goes "the long way around." Basically, if you pilot your product for innovators, nail it for early adopters, and scale it for the early majority, then you create maximum building of market awareness; you make smart, timely investments relative to market readiness; you maintain pricing and margins; and you avoid the commodity trap for as long as possible. That's the path to prosperity and one that avoids the classic strategy traps.

14. The Pre-Startup Checklist

I'm going to define the core difference between startup and pre-startup using a single word: commitment. Commitment means that the entrepreneur and founding team have taken a real risk to make the business happen. They are clearly and unequivocally *in*. It's Dodge City or Bust. Without commitment, the venture will remain stuck in pre-startup mode—as an idea that will never be actualized.

For example, I recently had coffee with an old colleague who wanted to talk about his new "startup." He had written a business plan, registered a domain name, and was seeking advice on raising capital and building the technology. He was still working at his day job, where he planned to stay while building on the idea in his spare time. As we talked, I could tell that what he really wanted was someone with whom he could discuss the idea—to explore it further and get another perspective. He was still just trying it on and not yet fully committed.

You can always tell if someone is committed to a new venture by his or her actions. Have they taken a significant risk such as quitting their day job or putting their own money into it? Are they excitedly and constantly talking about the opportunity? Are people rallying around their cause and vision? These are all great signs of commitment—and that's when you know you're in startup mode. With them, a new business can be born and has a chance of success. Without them, you're still in pre-startup or it's a non-starter.

Choosing the Right Customer

There's a popular view among technology startups that a smart business strategy is to build a product that's designed for the leading industry giant to acquire. It usually sounds something like this: "We're building the next-generation router that Cisco will need to add to its product line. Our strategy is to build the product, get them to adopt it, and ultimately have them buy us out."

On the surface, this is a classic textbook entrepreneurial strategy. Build a product for the leading company in the space to buy. But like a lot of things in life, just because this view is popular, doesn't mean it's right. In fact, gearing your strategy towards the leading industry giant goes against the principles of lifecycle strategy and you shouldn't do it. Here's why and how to choose a better strategy.

When a company early in its lifecycle stage targets its business strategy towards selling to the industry-leading giant to acquire, it's usually targeting an aging company. Yes, the targeted acquirer has plenty of cash, a listing on the NYSE, and a global footprint, but it has also long outgrown its entrepreneurial roots. It's a lot like a dinosaur, resting on its past accomplishments and no longer viable in a changing world. Its own customers are mostly late majority/laggard clients too. As a result, it is no longer in touch with where the market is headed. Sure, they can talk the talk at industry conferences but when you get down to it, they've lost touch with future growth opportunities.

Therefore, when a startup designs the product based on feedback from this lumbering giant, the product will be dated and poorly conceived and will miss the mark entirely. The seemingly powerful company has many interests operating within it that provide conflicting advice and express different, competing needs. "We need the product to be hip and cool for the next generation;" "No, we need the product to fit within our existing infrastructure;" and "Really, we need it to be validated and accepted by our channel partners" are all voices you're likely to hear.

The small startup is betting everything that the large potential acquirer will continue to execute on its stated strategy and not be derailed by a bad macro-economy or eclipsed by new technologies. While the giant may even have the startup's best interests at heart, that's not worth a wooden nickel if and when the giant is compelled to adapt to market changes, cut staff, and restructure. The likely outcome to this scenario is that the startup builds a product that one very large company says it wants but doesn't really need. That will probably translate to the rest of the market too. Having the stamp of approval from the industry leader doesn't help at all if the surrounding conditions have shifted.

A superior strategic approach for our small startup is to initially ignore the late majority/laggard client and instead find those innovative, cutting-edge users. Choose instead to collaborate with the market innovators and pilot the product for them. Show thought leadership, be a disruptor to the status quo, and find a better, easier way of doing things. Then move up the product/market/execution lifecycle and leverage your hard-earned thought leadership and innovator endorsements to nail the product for early adopters. You'll know you've nailed it when the early adopters purchase the product and then come back for more. Why? Because the product is meeting their needs. It's producing positive and desired results. While it's pretty easy to sell anything once, nothing gives an endorsement like a follow-on contract or a contract extension. Once you've nailed it, you then begin to scale the product for the early majority clients by standardizing, adding new line extensions, and increasing the product margin. It's a race now to be a niche market leader.

Just about at this point, the former startup will become a visible and desirable acquisition target for the original targeted acquirer. Why?

Because it did the exact opposite of what the aging giant would have requested! The giant now desperately needs the former startup because it is dominating its niche; it shows good margins, cash flow, entrepreneurial zeal, and thought leadership; and it seems to know where the market is headed. All these are things the late majority/laggard acquirer once seemed to have in abundance but no longer does. As a result (and if the startup still wants to sell), the acquirer will write a really large check for the pleasure.

By aligning the product/market/execution lifecycles in this way, a company gives itself a higher probability of success with the same companies it initially consciously ignored. It's counterintuitive, but that's what really works.

Here's a recent example of a company navigating the product/market/ execution lifecycles the right way. You may have heard of a company called Square Inc. Square is a mobile payment solution company that allows anyone to accept credit card payments using their mobile phone. In just over a year since its launch, the company had nearly $1 billion in processed payments. It has recently accepted an undisclosed investment from Visa, the leading credit card processor. The insider consensus is that, if Square continues to execute its strategy, it will revolutionize how we pay for things in the real world. It could be as disruptive to payments as iTunes was to music. How did this all happen in such a short amount of time?

The story of how Square came to life is a great one[9]. Square was created by Jack Dorsey, who also happens to be the co-founder and executive chairman of Twitter (but that's a different story). When you learn the story of Square, it becomes clear that Jack didn't start out to revolutionize the payments industry. His original goal was much more modest. Dorsey's former boss and good friend (and eventual co-founder) Jim McKelvey lost a sale for his hand-blown glass because he had no way of accepting credit cards. The problem was one many people had: The barriers to setting yourself up to accept credit card payments were too high. So Dorsey set about to see if he could create a better system.

The company focused its early product prototypes on the needs of the innovator clients—people like McKelvey who were avid smartphone users and had a business need to accept credit cards but weren't served by the status quo. As the company proved its concept, it began to show great thought leadership, point out flaws in the traditional credit card

<hr>

[9] Steven Truong, "Jack Dorsey on the History of Twitter and Square." *The Unofficial Stanford Blog* (May 2011). Retrieved from: http://tusb.stanford.edu/2011/05/jack-dorsey-on-the-history-of-twitter-and-square.html.

processing space, and predict how that space would change in the rapid shift to a mobile world. The company began to ship free card readers (little white "squares" that fit in most smartphones) to its early adopter clients. With a fanatical focus on design and user friendliness, they really nailed it for those clients, who became passionate, raving fans. Articles began to appear in metropolitan areas with stories about taco truck vendors and massage therapists using this strange little payment device on their iPhones. A new payment cult was born.

Right now, the company is moving into scale mode. It's filling out its board, creating industry alliances with companies like Visa, extending its product capabilities to support iPads and repeat purchases. We can expect to see new competitors emerge in the coming months and the company starting to increase its marketing and branding expenditures to capture the early majority clients—most of whom haven't heard about Square yet, but will soon.

Think about that for a moment. Square is revolutionizing the mobile payments space and they didn't start out by building a product for industry giants like Visa or PayPal. Instead, they designed a compelling solution for those unserved by the status quo—artists, taco truck vendors, and massage therapists! Because they piloted and nailed it for these innovator and early adopter clients, the industry giants such as Visa are now feeling afraid, knocking at their doors, and trying to get a piece of the action. And they *should* feel threatened because Square is ready to tap into a whole new market—allowing anyone with a mobile phone to get paid.

Imagine what would have happened if Square had followed popular strategic advice and tried to create a product for the industry giants to bid on and acquire. They would have gone to these behemoths and said, "We're designing a new mobile payments solution for you. What features and functions should it have?" They would have been bogged down in designing a product for the status quo, not for the next wave of innovative change. The product would have been clunky and it would have attempted to meet the needs of too many conflicting interests. It would have met the needs of the past, not the emerging needs of the future. It would never be where it is today. And although your business is probably in a different market, the principles that apply to it are exactly the same.

Customer-Driven Development

Within high-tech entrepreneurship circles today, "customer-driven development" or "sell, design, build" is all the rage. These approaches have been popularized by thought leaders such as Stephen Blank, author of *Four Steps to the Epiphany*; Eric Reis, author of *The Lean Startup*, and Frank Robinson of SyncDev, Inc. in Santa Barbara, California. It's worth commenting on how these approaches fit into the pre-startup checklist and the product/market/execution lifecycle scheme we're discussing.

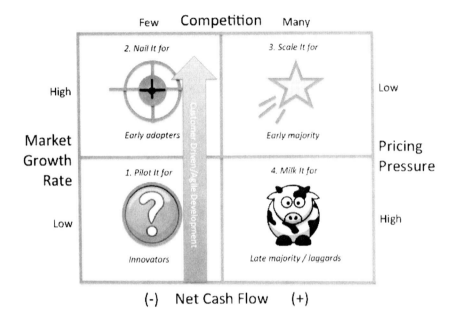

Figure 34. Customer-driven/agile development and lifecycle strategy.

Essentially, what the customer-driven development school recommends is that an entrepreneur go as far as possible from the start of quadrant 1 (Pilot it for Innovators) to the top of quadrant 2 (Nail it for Early Adopters) by interviewing, researching, and selling customers in advance before the product development process begins.

In other words, customer-driven development tries to limit the cost, risk, and time investment of making poor product or market decisions between the Pilot It and Nail It stages. They are looking for a good product/market fit before the development process begins. If they can discover what the thought leaders really value and what the early adopters' true spending priorities are before development begins, this lowers the risk and increases the probability of meeting those needs. Development can become more focused and demand is established before any real money is spent on development.

Agile software development is a product development method that aligns very closely with a customer-driven philosophy. Agile, or iterative, development is a process of taking real-time data from actual use of the product and quickly iterating changes using short release cycles to develop a better product that meets the needs of target customers. Fundamentally, agile is a product development method that attempts to better manage changing requirements; avoid long release cycles; and produce live, working, tested software that has real business value. In an early-stage startup, using an agile approach can help a company quickly and cost-effectively navigate the Pilot It to Nail It stages by eliminating the guesswork, long product release cycles, and overhead involved in trying to do a big product design up front. In larger companies with existing products in scale mode, using agile is an attempt to better meet user requirements, based on data and customer feedback, and to turn that knowledge more quickly into new product features and extensions.

Having built several successful high-tech products and run agile development teams, I can say that I am a big fan and believer in both approaches. They go hand in hand. Their real but unstated goal is to help a company navigate up the path to prosperity more quickly and cost-effectively. These approaches can help verify that your thinking is sound, that demand is there and you've uncovered a proven market opportunity. Additionally, having evidence that your entrepreneurial vision is baked in the cold, hard light of reality can make all the difference in raising the capital you need. These are sound methods and they fit perfectly well into the strategy lifecycle scheme.

The truth is that there are many other methods that can also help you quickly navigate the path to prosperity. Customer-driven can work. So can vision-driven. For example, I don't believe Steve Jobs had ever done a day of listening to focus groups in his entire life. Instead, he had that rare ability to envision something entirely new, intuitively understand the needs of his target customers even before they did, and bring his vision to the world in surprising and beautiful ways. No external customer-driven development of the iPad would have worked because customers would have had no frame of reference for it. Walt Disney was the same way. He had a powerful vision and followed his own instincts about what families really valued that wasn't being provided by other amusement parks at the time. He created magical experiences that no one was expecting. The point is that there are many ways to develop a product but the fundamentals of strategy should always be the same: You must go the long way around the path and create the product/market fit in the right sequence.

The Pre-Startup Checklist

Before a startup really launches, you should have a checklist of critical items in place. These items have nothing to do with writing a business plan or forming the articles of incorporation. In line with the old saying, "well begun is half done," without these basic requirements, the venture won't get off to a successful start. Even worse, ignoring this checklist can lead to your investing a lot of capital, time, and energy—only to find out that you're doing the wrong thing, with the wrong team, at the wrong time.

1. Align Vision and Values

Don't overlook the importance of this. Misalignment is a real deal breaker. The bottom line is that every element in the venture needs to align with the founding team's vision and values. This goes hand in hand with commitment because it's impossible to be truly committed to something that's not aligned with your vision and values. Imagine an entrepreneur who has a strong desire to make money. He or she starts a business in a cut-throat market where the money is good but most competitors engage in shady practices. In order to compete, this entrepreneur must sacrifice honesty and integrity and rationalize this inauthentic choice ("I'll suck it up, do this for a few years, and come out with a boatload of cash. Then I can do some good in the world"). This entrepreneur is delusional. It costs a tremendous amount of energy and effort to go against your vision and values, even in the short run. The result is great stress, inner turmoil, and conflict. Even if the entrepreneur does hit a big financial payoff in the future, the resulting internal entropy is extreme. In most cases, these ventures end in a broken sense of self, destroyed relationships, and toxic addictions. Deep passion, commitment, and alignment are all essential to a healthy, successful business.

2. Know Your Customers' Pain

In pre-startup mode, it's most critical that the founding team understands the pain or problems of the target market. Too many ventures launch without a clear understanding of the customer pain or need that they are trying to solve. In my opinion, if there is no customer pain, there is no business gain. For example, I was invited to lunch last month with a funded startup. They had built a mobile application for consumers to record and share their drink purchases when out at restaurants and bars. They had spent about $150K of investor money building the app. Their problem was that consumers weren't adopting it and they wanted to know how to pivot the strategy.

I asked them to describe the pain or need of their target audience and they couldn't do it. "Pain? There is no pain here," they said, "it's just a fun app to have." I pointed out that even the most fun or frivolous app, if successful, has solved some underlying pain or need. In this company's case, the real target audience was probably the bars and restaurants that had the pain of not having enough customers, or revenue per customer, and needed a solution. If they had spent time investigating their target audience needs more closely and identifying the real pain and spending priorities up front, they would have saved a lot of time, energy, and capital.

Your pre-startup venture doesn't need a formal 40-page business plan. It does, however, need to be able to answer some basic questions about who the target customers are, what their pain or need is, how the product will solve it (and how this will be measured), why the venture is truly important, and why you are unique or different from the practical alternatives. You'll also want to have a good understanding of the likely customer acquisition costs, product pricing, major cost centers, lifetime value of the customer, how customers want to buy the product or service, and from whom they prefer to buy it.

All of this information takes focused energy and effort to gather up front. Having gathered this information early on shows that the entrepreneur is serious about the venture, has thought things through clearly, knows what to look for and measure, and can better adapt along the way. When researching the opportunity, you should of course assess the product and market lifecycles as well. If the business is too late to market, the market isn't ready yet, the market is too hard to service effectively, and so on, the business should not launch rather than embark in a strategic folly. The alternative is blindly forging ahead only to waste $150K of your friends' and family's money. As a wise man once said, the plan is useless but the planning is priceless.

3. Get the Right People on the Bus

In addition to having aligned vision and values, it's obviously critical that your venture have, or be able to get, the resources it needs to execute. These resources include people, technology, customers, and capital, as well as the expertise required to start and grow the business. While capital can feel like the scarcest or most important resource, it's really not. The truth is that all resources and expertise flow from the people involved. If you have the right people, you can uncover the right opportunity, build the right technology, attract the right customers, and get the capital you need to scale. Without the right people, none of this will occur. In his book *Good to Great*, management consultant Jim Collins makes this very clear. Collins talks about "Who's on the bus?" as a metaphor for recognizing that what you do isn't nearly as important as who is involved. In short, the greatest strategy in the world doesn't amount to a hill of beans unless you have the right set of people who can execute.

4. Don't Wear Cement Shoes

There's another critical process you should engage in before launching a business—and that's doing an internal entropy scan. As you're talking, planning, and researching the business, how are the internal friction or energy drains within you and the team? Are people getting more excited as you investigate the business idea further? Is commitment building? Do you trust and respect your potential co-founders and team members? Do they trust and respect you? Can you complement each other without causing a lot of unnecessary, energy-draining friction? Are these the people with whom you want to go into battle? If the answer is "no," you've got a sign of unhealthy entropy and you should not underestimate its impact. My advice: Pull yourself out or cull out the friction-causing team members before the venture gets started.

As you perform an entropy scan within the team, don't forget to include personal issues that can either help or hinder the success of the venture. For example, if mission-critical founding members have a high level of friction and discord in their personal lives, this will have a magnified negative impact on the venture. Maybe they are suffering through a health issue, dealing with a toxic divorce, or in conflict with an unsupportive spouse. In all these situations, personal friction and entropy will rise, making it much harder to maintain the all-consuming focus required for a new business venture. On the other hand, a founding team member with the right style, skills, vision, dedication, and passion and who has a supportive family can be worth their weight in gold, even if they've never done a startup venture before.

So be mindful of the sources of friction surrounding the founding team's lives and families, just as you would be mindful of them within the business itself. A larger company can compensate for contingencies and personal issues but a new venture is tied directly to the available energy and mental and emotional capabilities of the founding team. It's a long journey ahead and you can't possibly plan for every contingency, but if you notice high entropy at the start, save yourself the time, capital, headache, and failure in advance. There will be enough to deal with after the business has launched and you don't want to start out wearing cement shoes.

All Systems Go

To summarize the pre-startup checklist, an entrepreneur or founding team needs to prove real commitment; have a strong sense of the underlying problem that the market wants solved (and sense that they can solve it profitably); feel alignment between the venture and their vision and values; get the right people on the bus; and have low entropy in the system. If these elements are not all in place, the founders need to go back to the drawing board and find a venture that does meet those requirements. If they are and the founders follow the product/market/execution lifecycles in the right sequence, they'll have a real shot at success.

15. The Strategy Map: Where Are You Now?

The picture of strategic success occurs where all three lifecycles—product, market, and execution—are closely aligned. It looks like this and creates a Strategy Map that we can use to choose the right strategy:

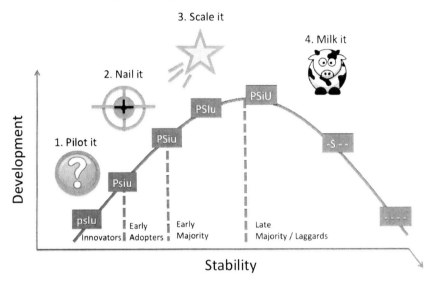

Figure 35. The Strategy Map.

Figuring out your strategy is much like figuring out how to get from point A to point B on a map. Obviously, the first thing you need to do when traveling anywhere is to identify where you are starting. Strategy is the same. The real strategic question is not "what should you do next?" but first, "where are you now?"

Here's how you figure that out and, by default, determine what you should do next in your strategy. As you look at

Figure 35 above, place each of your products (or business unit groupings of multiple products) where you think it most likely resides on the execution lifecycle curve. If you have multiple business units, place each of them where you think it currently resides.

For example, if your product is in the Nail It stage, where the business unit is making sales but hasn't yet developed its systems to scale, then place it in the Nail It section after Psiu and before PSiu. Or, if you have one product that's still in concept mode, place it in the Pilot It section, after psIu and before Psiu.

Next, do an entropy scan of each business unit. Is it acting in a sluggish or friction-filled manner? If so, then move it off of the execution lifecycle curve and lower towards the Stability axis. Do this to give a visual sense of any entropy occurring in the system. That is, products or business units with high entropy will act more stable, stuck, or stalled in their execution, so place them nearer the Stability axis. If there's little entropy and high integration, keep those products and business units on the execution lifecycle curve.

Once the products or business units are placed in their correct locations on the map, the basic rule of thumb is to work in this order:

1. Move each product/business unit that's *below* the execution lifecycle curve back *up* to the execution lifecycle curve (or sell it, or kill it).

2. Move each product/business unit that is *on* the curve to the next stage of its lifecycle.

The reason for the first step is that those products/business units have high entropy. As you know, high entropy prevents execution and so these product/business units can't move forward and execute until the entropy is lowered. How you realign those business units and lower the entropy is the subject of the next part of this book. For now, just recognize that if a product/business unit is suffering from a high amount of friction, stuckness, or other energy drains, those drains first need to be removed before the product/business unit can move forward swiftly. The concept of moving a product/business unit that's off the execution lifecycle curve back onto that curve symbolizes the energy, focus, and effort required to get that product/business unit to move forward to the next stage of its lifecycle. It can't move forward yet. It first has to move "up," then forward.

If a product/business unit already has low entropy, then it's ready and capable of moving forward to the next stage of the execution lifecycle. Now it's a matter of following the next set of strategic steps as identified on the map. For example, if a business unit currently exists on the execution lifecycle curve in the early Nail It stage, then its strategic steps become crystal clear by just reading the map. First, make sure that you are nailing the product for early adopter clients. You should have a relentless focus on proving that you solve the core customer pain or problem. Once that is accomplished, your next set of strategic steps is to stabilize how you sell and service that product while shifting your sales and marketing focus to early majority clients, and so on up the curve. By following the stages on the Strategy Map, you avoid strategic follies and give yourself the highest probability of success.

Below is a simple but real example of how to use the Strategy Map to your advantage. This map was created during a Strategic Alignment Workshop that I facilitated with the ten-person senior management team of a venture-backed software as a service (SaaS) provider. At the time of the workshop, the company was generating $5M in annual revenues with about 50 employees and several hundred enterprise customers. The company has one legacy product (Product A) and one new product (Product B). Its goal was to get to $20M in sales in three years. After performing a collaborative team wide assessment of the company, the market, and its products,

Figure 36 shows how the map presented itself.

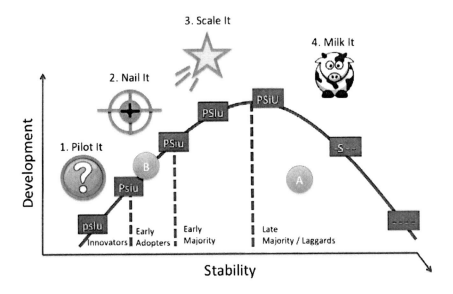

Figure 36. The Strategy Map in action (part 1).

Here's a snapshot of the map. This company has one legacy product (A) that represents nearly 90 percent of its revenue. This product was operating in maintenance mode on the aging side of the execution lifecycle. It had pretty high entropy surrounding it, exemplified by a lack of passion for the product, poor systems, the absence of a clear sense of ownership, and an inability to prioritize and execute on new feature development. It was subsisting but not thriving.

The company has a new product (B) that is generating a lot of excitement and traction in the marketplace. It now exists in the Nail It phase and the company is passionate and excited about its potential. There is great leadership and a clear product development roadmap around this product and it is winning sales from key early adopter clients. Based on this map, the strategy became very clear.

First of all, the company recognized that it needed to fix the core problems in Product A. It simply couldn't afford to let its cash cow reach the end of its life on the current trajectory, nor did it make sense to try to sell it off to a strategic acquirer. Product A needed to get reinvigorated and move back up to the execution lifecycle and we created a plan to do that. After moving up, the company felt they could do a good job of selling and servicing existing accounts, maintaining the product, and using the proceeds to fund the development of Product B. That is, they weren't going to try to reinvigorate it to the growing side of the execution lifecycle and really scale it up, but just treat it like a cash cow to fund new business development. It needed some more TLC, but not the Ritz Carlton treatment.

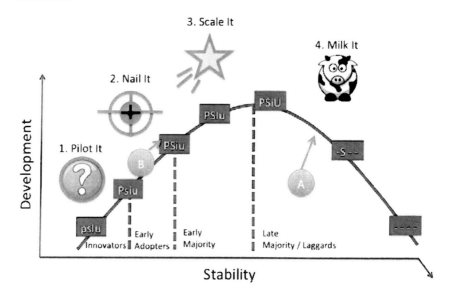

Figure 37. The Strategy Map in action (part 2).

For Product B, the company realized that it needed to shift two things. One, they decided not to pursue early majority clients until they had better systems in place to support them. Instead, they would continue to sell to early adopter clients who were better suited to helping the company refine its product/market fit and didn't have the same service level requirements as the next stage. Two, they needed to invest much more aggressively in systems and staffing to support the next stage of the lifecycle growth curve. The collective epiphany was "we've got to nail it before we can scale it."

So this is the essence of strategy. You identify where you are in the product, market, and execution lifecycles; you avoid strategic follies; and you execute fast. In Part IV, we're going to cover how you execute quickly by aligning the organization for superior performance.

Lex Sisney

Part IV - Execute Fast

16. The Physics of Fast Execution

Ahhhh—momentum!

Isn't it a great feeling when you finally have it working in your favor? When all the pieces have fallen into place, at the right time, allowing your company to speed towards its objective . . . it's epic. It's like riding a freight train that's roaring down the tracks—and you just keep picking up speed.

Of course, when your company has no momentum, it's just the opposite. It feels like, no matter what you do, you just can't get the train to move along. Things take too long to complete, people aren't on the same page, obstacles rear their heads at every turn, and even the best incentive plans don't seem to make a difference. It's frustrating.

So how do you create or re-create momentum in your organization so you can execute swiftly on the strategy? When faced with this question, it's easy to revert to popular management platitudes. You've probably heard that you must "communicate a clear vision," "create sound systems and processes," "offer compelling incentives," "set realistic expectations," "reward desired behavior," and so on. This advice is valuable but also misleading. Furthermore, its relative value is dependent on context and may not be the answer in every situation, all the time. To get real, lasting, universally applicable answers, you have to go deeper.

There is a secret to creating organizational momentum that has been hidden in plain sight for over 300 years. In his *Principia Mathematica Philosophiae Naturalis,* Isaac Newton laid down the basic laws that govern the movement of physical objects in our universe[10]. Ever since, these have been popularly known as Newton's three laws of motion. Physicists and engineers must still reckon with them to design just about anything that moves or is impacted by the motion of other objects. What's surprising is that, even though an organization is not a physical object, these same three laws can also be used to better understand and influence the momentum of an organization. In other words, Newton's three laws of motion can be used to understand the speed and direction of organizations of all sizes, much like rockets traveling to Mars. Once you understand the basics, it's easy to spot these laws all around you and learn to work with—rather than against—them to increase the momentum of your organization.

---

[10] Isaac Newton, *Philosophiae Naturalis Principia Mathematica, Volume 1; Volume 3* (Munich: Bavarian State Library, 1760).

Lex Sisney

Newton's Three Laws of Motion

Let's do a thought experiment. Imagine that you're standing in the middle of a racquetball court. At your feet is a soccer ball. First, notice how the soccer ball just tends to sit there. That's called inertia. In order to get the ball to do something, you have to apply a force to it. In this case, you give it a kick and the ball rolls along the floor, bounces off the wall, and careens in another direction before coming to rest again. Next, you walk and retrieve the ball and bring it back to the center of the court, place it on the floor, and this time, you give it a really hard kick. What happens? The ball rolls even faster across the floor, bounces off the wall with more power, and travels further in a new direction than the first kick. In essence, you just experienced all three of Newton's laws of motion.

Newton's three laws of motion will shed light on the speed and direction of your organization. If you want to move your organization forward quickly in a chosen direction, you should understand these laws and how they apply to business execution.

The First Law of Motion

Newton's first law of motion is about inertia. Inertia is a recognition that an object will tend to do what it's been doing, unless acted upon by an imbalanced or outside force. In our thought experiment, that's why the ball tends to stay at rest in the middle of the floor until you do something, like give it a kick. Inertia works in both ways, however. Once the ball is in motion from the kick, it tends to stay in motion too, until an outside force such as gravity, friction, or a wall acts upon it. Once the ball comes to rest, it will remain at rest until it is acted upon by another force.

Although an organization isn't a simple object like a ball, you can still use the lens of inertia to view it. In other words, an organization will tend to continue to do what it's been doing unless acted upon by another force. That is, if your organization is slowed, stymied, or stuck, it will continue to act that way unless you do something to change it. And the greater the inertia, the greater the effort required at getting it to move in a new direction. On the other hand, if your organization is currently experiencing a lot of momentum, then like a train roaring down the tracks, it will be hard to slow down. Inertia can work in your favor too.

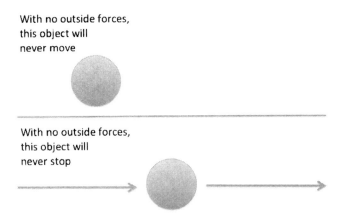

With no outside forces, this object will never move

With no outside forces, this object will never stop

Figure 38. Newton's first law of motion.

The Second Law of Motion

Newton's second law of motion is about the relationship between force, mass, and acceleration. In our thought experiment, when you kicked the ball harder, it had more acceleration and went further. There's an equation in physics that explains this: $F=MA$ (Force equals Mass times Acceleration). Basically, $F=MA$ tells us that if you take two objects of the same mass and hit one with force, you'll have acceleration. If you hit the other with more force, you'll have more acceleration. That's why if you were to take two identical soccer balls and kick one really hard, it would accelerate to a certain speed and travel a set distance. Kick the other one less hard and it will accelerate to a slower speed and travel less distance.

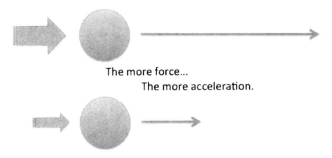

The more force...
The more acceleration.

Figure 39. Newton's second law of motion.

While any frustrated CEO would love to kick their organization in the
ass to get it to accelerate, it's obvious that that's not how things work. But
why? Why can't a CEO, a teacher, or a parent apply a force of change to
the organization and make it move as quickly and easily as a kicked ball? If
F=MA, then why don't your kids pick up their toys when you tell them
to? Why doesn't your sales team respond to the force of your incentive
plan? Why won't the market readily respond to the appeal of your
advertising?

The answer is not (entirely) that an organization isn't a physical object
like a ball. The answer is also this: Mass is not size or volume. Mass is
resistance to change. So the reason an organization, or a person, or a
market is relatively hard or easy to move is its inertia or resistance to
change. If the organization has a high mass or resistance to change, it will
be very difficult to get it to alter its behavior. If the resistance is low, on
the other hand, change can come easily. Just because a Fortune 500
company is really "large," does not mean its mass or resistance is
necessarily big. Or just because a family of four is relatively "small"
doesn't mean that its mass is automatically light.

Here's an example to show why mass is resistance to change and not
size or volume. The United States of America is a very large, complex
organization. Imagine that you have been elected president. You want to
implement changes that you believe will benefit all. However, there are
over 300 million people, each with different needs, wants, desires, and
perceptions, who are all represented by different politicians, who are in
turn supported by different corporations and political action groups. Your
legislative agenda is seen as beneficial to some segments and as a terrible
loss to others. Therefore, the mass is very high. Even though you're the
president, it's very, very hard to push your agenda forward because the
resistance to change is so great.

There's a saying in Washington: "Never lose the opportunity of a
good crisis." What does this mean? When there's a crisis, the normal
resistance to change is lowered because the system is under threat. When
this occurs, it becomes much easier to get new legislation passed. For
example, after the 9/11 crisis in the United States, new legislation called
the Patriot Act was quickly passed. This legislation radically curtailed civil
and constitutional liberties and would have been unthinkable without a
crisis that first reduced the resistance to change.

I'm not advocating that you create crises to get your organization to
do something differently. Rather, I'm making the point that mass is not
size or volume but resistance to change—and even a very large
organization, such as a country, will move quickly in a new direction if the
resistance to change is low enough. Once the organization gets moving in

that new direction, it will tend to stay on that course until another force causes it to stop or change.

The Third Law of Motion

Newton's third law of motion recognizes that for every action, there is an equal and opposite reaction. That's why when the soccer ball in our experiment hits the wall, it careens off in the opposite direction from which it struck. If the ball is coming quickly into the wall, it will travel far in the opposite direction. If it's coming slowly into the wall, it will travel less distance in the opposite direction. Action and reaction are the essence of the third law of motion.

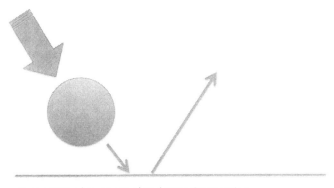

Every action has an equal and opposite reaction

Figure 40. Newton's third law of motion.

Therefore, when you're implementing change in one area of your organization, there will always be an equal and opposite reaction in another. If you're not careful, the opposite reaction can also slow down the speed and direction of your organization.

For example, imagine that your business is expanding rapidly. This is something you've wanted for a long time and you've worked very hard at it. You've finally got the momentum you were seeking but guess what happens next? Faced with the new growth, the business' administrative systems and people start falling apart and must be managed to keep pace. That's an equal and opposite reaction. If you don't manage the reaction well, it will act as a drag on your momentum. Or, with all the work and effort you've put into the business, your family life is stretched thin. If you can't find a way to restore harmony, the family system will suffer from an equal and opposite reaction to your booming business.

Gathering the Mass

The secret to accelerating momentum—and doing it sustainably—lies in how the organization's mass is managed. That is, if the mass is manageable (i.e. cohesive and unified), then it's easy to apply a force of change and get the organization to do something new. Within organizational dynamics, the challenge in managing mass is that resistance to change is scattered throughout the organization. Mass lies within the individuals making the decisions, those doing the work, and those who can help, hinder, or influence the results—all of which naturally have different needs and perspectives. Therefore, no matter how much or what type of force you attempt to apply, when the organizational mass is widely dispersed (in other words, not cohesive and aligned), there's nothing that can be leveraged to effectively push or pull against the organizational inertia.

Think of it like this: The reason that your organization doesn't behave like a soccer ball is because its mass is scattered all about, more like shattered pieces of glass than a single object. With such a dispersal of mass, no matter how much of a force of change you try to apply, it won't be very responsive.

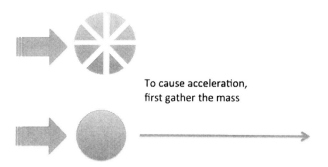

To cause acceleration, first gather the mass

Figure 41. To create acceleration, first gather the mass.

If it were possible to gather the pieces of glass and glue them back together—in other words, to make them behave like a ball again, you would reduce resistance to change. You could hit your organization with a force, such as a decision or a directive, and it would tend to rapidly accelerate in a new direction.

Aligning the Organization to Increase Momentum

In 1993 I was a college student in St. Paul, Minnesota. I drove a twenty-year-old canary yellow Toyota Corolla with bald tires, a broken heater, and a misaligned chassis. Because my spending priorities then were the necessities of college life (pizza, beer, girls, and rent), I never invested in making the car safe to drive. Navigating that car on the icy roads of thirty-below Minnesota winters required a certain ability to go with the flow. But eventually, my refusal to replace the tires and align the chassis caught up with me. Driving late one winter night ... it's easy to guess what happened. Wipe out. Crash. Car totaled.

Thankfully, no one was hurt.

I share this story because in one way a misaligned car is like a misaligned business – it's a recipe for a crash. In my late twenties to my mid-thirties, I received some important lessons on the value of organizational alignment. After facing many challenges around alignment, I ultimately led two companies into compound annual growth rates (CAGR) exceeding 5,000 percent per year—from startup to $4M and $12M in two and four years, respectively. While this may be chump change to some entrepreneurs, these periods of rapid growth were priceless learning for me. They also provide a valuable lesson that's applicable to companies of all sizes and at all lifecycle stages.

In order to get that kind of exponential growth, I didn't have to fight, cajole, or struggle for years. Instead, the leadership team and I figured out how to create the right internal and external alignment for growth to occur. If you can get the internal and external alignment right for your own business, you'll dramatically increase its probability of thriving and executing very quickly. I'm not guaranteeing 5,000 percent CAGR. In fact, I'm not even recommending you try for that—it's much wiser to shoot for more sustainable rates of growth. The act of creating alignment, however, is essential to every business. Get it right and your company can execute swiftly and powerfully. Get it wrong and you won't get back on the growth curve until you do get it right. Alignment is the key.

Alignment is what keeps your organization's mass (M) on track, cohesive, and manageable. There are four basic organizational subsystems through which you accomplish this: (1) the organization's Vision and Values, (2) the organizational Structure or design, (3) the decision-making and implementation Process, and (4) the People and teams involved. Think of these subsystems like a corral or a boundary that helps to keep the organization unified, cohesive, and coherent in both vision and action. I refer to these subsystems together as the Execution Diamond:

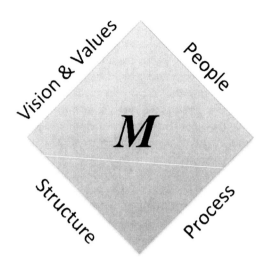

Figure 42. The Execution Diamond.

Your objective is to align each of these subsystems with your chosen strategy as it evolves. When all of these elements come together, you're going to have a much higher probability of executing fast and therefore catching your growth wave. This should make a lot of sense. Envision a company with the right strategy and business model for the current market conditions. The core team shares the same vision and values. They all want to end up in the same destination and have the same boundaries on what is and isn't acceptable behavior. There's a structure in place that assigns authority and accountability for the work that needs to be done. The team has a sound process to consistently make good decisions and implement them fast. And talented, passionate people are in the organization because they sense an opportunity and are intrinsically motivated by the work to be done. If you had all these things, how could you not be successful?

All this means that if you want a fast-moving organization with minimal friction and obstacles along the way, you should make it your priority to create this alignment before taking action. It also means that you should never take action in a misaligned environment—unless that action is aimed at aligning it first. You will spare yourself the headaches and sleepless nights, as well as save a tremendous amount of time, energy, and resources. In the next four chapters, I will show you how to align each of the four sides of the Execution Diamond in order of importance.

17. Aligning Vision and Values

There are few things that will destroy momentum within an organization like a conflict in vision and values. Before I explain why this is so, what to do if you have a conflict of vision and values among your employees, and how to align or realign a shared sense of vision and values, allow me to define what I mean by "vision and values" in the first place.

Vision is the destination or ultimate outcome towards which the organization is ideally collectively working. For example, imagine that you're a sea captain. Vision would be the destination and outcomes you're seeking from a successful voyage. Are you sailing to Tahiti or Vancouver? And what do you hope to gain from such a voyage? Knowledge? Treasure? Experience? Or simply a ride to a new place? If vision is the destination, then values are the norms of behavior that are deemed acceptable during the voyage. What kind of ship would you run? Would it be clean, orderly, and tight? Or would you sail like a loose but creative band of pirates? How the work is done reveals the values you espouse.

The same concepts hold true for your company. To be effective, an organization needs a shared and compelling vision so that everyone buys into where the organization is sailing and why. The crew has bought into the vision; they understand their role on the voyage; and they're eager and determined to make it happen. They must also embody a shared code of values so that everyone is clear on the modes of acceptable behavior and, more importantly, what isn't acceptable behavior—the kind that will get you walking the plank. Without a compelling vision and clear, authentic, and sustainable values, no company will get very far very fast.

What Happens if There's a Conflict of Vision and Values

A true conflict of vision and values is an extreme situation that can't be negotiated. That is, if an individual has a vision and values conflicting with the organization's, the individual must go (yes, that means leave the organization). Intuitively, this should make sense. For how can two groups of people get along and work together if they want to head in opposite directions or don't value the same conduct? For example, if a couple no longer share the same vision and values for their relationship, no amount of counseling is going to save it. It's best for both parties to part ways and find partners who do share their vision and values. Likewise, if two company co-founders have a genuine conflict of vision and values, one should leave or get bought out or they should both agree to shut the company down. The organization is just not going to make it while that conflict exists.

On a global scale, we have seen plenty of conflicts of vision and values in action. Communism and capitalism are perhaps the most flagrant 20th-century examples. In cases like this, if one imposes itself on the other, the resistance to change is so great that this usually results in war. Conflicting vision and values are the major reason why peace between Israel and Palestine is so hard to negotiate. Both sides have a fundamentally different vision and values around coexistence and no peace treaties, walls, terrorism, or sanctions are going to bring them together. When large conflicts of this nature begin to dissolve, it's often the work of extraordinary leaders (think of the likes of Gandhi, Martin Luther King, and Nelson Mandela) who create a new, shared vision and values in the collective consciousness. These examples, unfortunately, are as rare as they are powerful.

Because it's so extreme, your best course of action when you suspect a potential conflict of vision and values is to prevent that conflict in advance. There's an old saying that when the head is rotten, it affects the whole body. Put another way, vision and values tend to flow from the top of the organization down. Therefore, you want to be extra vigilant that those in leadership positions have bought into a common vision and values and actually walk the talk. When this occurs, by their very presence, they naturally instill a shared vision and values and help to cascade them throughout the organization. Here's how you accomplish this.

How to Align Vision and Values

When it comes to aligning the team around a shared sense of vision and values, you obviously can't just write up a manifesto, post it around the office, and get everyone to buy in, walk the talk, and really get it. Instead, the company vision and values need to become the centerpiece of your day-to-day communications.

There's a saying that "effective leadership is the art of saying the same thing 1,000 different ways." When it comes to communicating with your employees about what's most important, your message needs to continually flow back to the vision and values of the organization. Why do we do what we do? Who do we serve and how are we making a positive difference? When are we at our best? How do we go about our daily work? What kind of behavior do we celebrate and what do we not tolerate? Of course it's not enough to talk the talk; you've got to walk it too and ensure that your team leaders are doing the same.

The legendary football coach Bill Walsh did this by using a simple matrix to help align the vision and values of the San Francisco 49ers in the 1980s. When Walsh joined the 49ers, he was a former college coach in his first year of coaching professional football. At the time, the 49ers were infamous for being perennial losers. Nothing in the organization seemed to go right. Walsh intuitively knew that if he was going to create a Super Bowl champion, then he would first have to change the culture by instilling in his players a new vision and a new set of values. The model he created is powerful in its insight and simplicity. The first step in using it is to place all of your current staff into one of four quadrants: those who share the vision and values and those who do not, and those who have high proficiency in their tasks (produce results) and those who do not.[11]

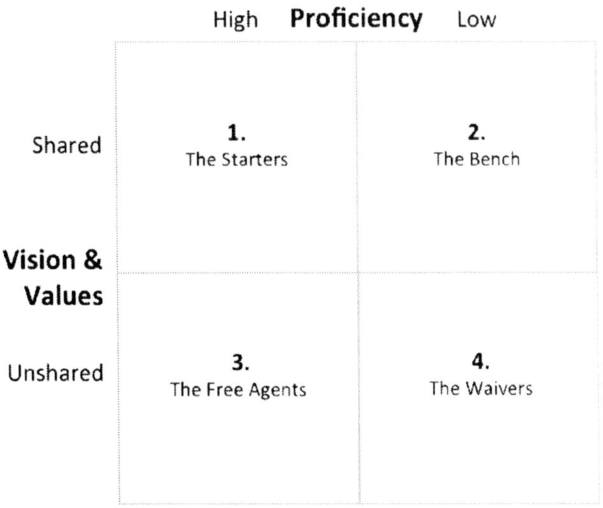

Figure 43. Who's on your team?

The Starters in quadrant 1 are those individuals who exemplify the best that your organization can be. They walk the talk. They embody the desired vision and values of your organization and, at the same time, they have a very high level of proficiency (e.g., their skill in sales, marketing, finance, programming, etc.). When it comes to managing starters, you want to develop their capabilities and career paths for the long term. This is a strategic investment and a smart one. Your job as manager is to help them cultivate their own leadership qualities and find the career path that is most engaging and rewarding to them. Celebrate and honor this group. Include them in strategic planning and the new hire process. They can set the tone and tempo for your entire organization.

---

[11] Lecture presented by former San Francisco 49er football player Brian Holloway at Big Speak, Inc. (Santa Barbara, California).

The Bench in quadrant 2 includes those individuals who exemplify the desired culture of your company but who don't perform at the same level of proficiency as the starters. When it comes to managing the bench, your job is to coach them and train them to improve their proficiency for the task at hand. Invest time, energy, and attention in this group for results today. It is relatively easy to develop competence in the short run but it is very, very challenging to develop character in the long run. You either have it or you don't. Therefore, value those in quadrant 2 and coach them in technical proficiency.

The Free Agents in quadrant 3 are those who perform technically at a very high level but who don't align with the company's vision and values. This is like a group of mercenaries. They are in the game only for themselves and everyone knows it. Be careful with this group. Use free agents sparingly and in areas that are non-critical for the business but require a specialized skill. At all costs, do not put free agents in leadership positions. If you do, this will have an adverse effect on the entire culture. When it comes to managing free agents, your job is to motivate and create incentives that reward short-term performance. Pay them cash on the barrelhead for a job well done. But do not attempt to win them over by offering a career path, an equity stake, or a leadership position that unduly influences others.

The Waivers in quadrant 4 include those who don't perform at a high level and don't share the desired vision and values of the company either. If this was a sports team, this is the group you'd place on the waiver wire and hope to trade to the competition. There's no real point in investing time, energy, and attention in improving skills or attempting to create a shared sense of vision and values. In other words, you can put lipstick on a pig, but it's still a pig. Do yourself and that person a favor: Help them find a new job with a different company that better aligns with their talents, vision, and values. You'll both be better off.

Using a simple model like this matrix will help you clarify your hiring strategy, as well as identify and quickly group the types of people in your organization and develop a short- and long-range plan to develop each one. It will also help you create a powerful organizational culture. Bill Walsh accomplished this in the 80s with the "49er way." Other great football dynasties such as the Steelers and Patriots also have their own clear cultural identity. The coaches, staff, and players can say "This is Steeler Football," and everyone knows what that means. People get it. It's communicated constantly and reinforced in individual organizational actions. Conversely, when an organization loses sight of its vision and values—like Hewlett Packard and the now almost forgotten "HP Way"—its organizational culture will suffer, impacting its business performance as well. Warren Buffet put it aptly in a recent Berkshire Hathaway shareholder letter: "Our final advantage is the hard-to-duplicate culture that permeates Berkshire ... in businesses, culture counts."

So as you go about growing your business, never forget this: Nothing creates greater misalignment in an organization and slows execution more than a conflict of vision and values. Therefore, attempt to avoid misalignment by being clear and committed to a powerful vision and authentic values up front. Fill leadership positions in your team with individuals who intrinsically share that same vision and values and make these the centerpiece of your communications and actions. If you can do this, and be committed to it over time, then your organization can build a thriving culture and accomplish great things indeed.

18. Aligning the Organizational Structure

I f I were to ask you a random and seemingly strange question, "Why does a rocket behave the way it does and how is it different from a parachute that behaves the way it does?" you'd probably say something like, "Well, duh, they're designed differently. One is designed to go fast and far and the other is designed to cause drag and slow an object in motion. Because they're designed differently, they behave differently." And you'd be correct. How something is designed controls how it behaves (if you doubt this, just try attaching an engine directly to a parachute and see what happens).

But if I were to ask you a similar question about your business, "Why does your business behave the way it does and how can you make it behave differently?" would you answer "design?" Very few people—even management experts—would. But the fact is that how your organization is designed determines how it performs. If you want to improve organizational performance, you'll need to change the organizational design. And the heart of organizational design is its structure.

Form Follows Function: The Principles of Organizational Structure

There's a saying in architecture and design that "form follows function." Put another way, the design of something should support its purpose. For example, take a minute and observe the environment you're sitting in, as well as the objects in it. Notice how everything serves a particular purpose. The purpose of a chair is to support a sitting human being, which is why it's designed the way it is. Great design means that something is structured in such a way that it allows it to serve its purpose very well. All of its parts are of the right type and placed exactly where they should be for their intended purpose. Poor design is just the opposite. Like a chair with an uncomfortable seat or an oddly measured leg, a poorly designed object just doesn't perform like you want it to.

Even though your organization is a complex adaptive system and not a static object, the same principles hold true for it. If the organization has a flawed design, it simply won't perform well. It must be structured (or restructured) to create a design that supports its function or business strategy.

What actually gives an organization its "shape" and controls how it performs are three things:

1. **The functions it performs,** or the core areas or activities in which the organization must engage to accomplish its strategy (e.g., Sales, Customer Service, Marketing, Accounting, Finance,

Operations, CEO, Admin, HR, Legal, PR, R&D, and
Engineering)

2. **The location of each function,** or where each function is placed
   in the organizational structure and how it interacts with other
   functions.

3. **The authority of each function within its domain,** or each
   function's ability to make decisions within its domain and to
   perform its activities without unnecessary encumbrance.

A sound organizational structure will make it unarguably clear what
each function (and ultimately each person) is accountable for. In addition,
the design must both support the current business strategy and allow the
organization to adapt to changing market conditions and customer needs
over time.

When you know what to look for, it's pretty easy to identify when an
organization's structure is out of whack. Imagine a company with an
existing cash cow business that is coming under severe pricing pressure.
Its margins are deteriorating quickly and the market is changing rapidly.
Everyone in the company knows that it must adapt or die. Its chosen
strategy is to continue to milk the cash cow (while it can) and use those
proceeds to invest in new verticals. On paper, it realigns some reporting
functions and allocates more budget to new business development units.
It holds an all-hands meeting to talk about the new strategy and the future
of the business. Confidence is high. The team is a good one. Everyone is
genuinely committed to the new strategy. They launch with gusto.

But here's the catch. Beneath the surface-level changes, the old power
structures remain. This is a common problem with companies at this
stage. The "new" structure is really just added to the old one, like a house
with an addition—and things get confusing. Who's responsible for which
part of the house? While employees genuinely want the new business
units to thrive, there's often a lack of clarity, authority, and accountability
around them. In addition, the new business units, which need freedom to
operate in startup mode, have to deal with an existing bureaucracy and old
ways of doing things. The CEO is generally oblivious to these problems
until late in the game. Everyone continues to pay lip service to the strategy
and the importance of the new business units but doubt, frustration, and a
feeling of ineptitude have already crept in. How this happens will become
clearer as you read on.

An organization's structure gets misaligned for many reasons. But the
most common one is simply inertia. The company gets stuck in an old
way of doing things and has trouble breaking free of the past. How did it

get this way to begin with? When an organization is in startup to early growth mode, the founder(s) control most of the core functions. The founding engineer is also the head of sales, finance, and customer service. As the business grows, the founders become a bottleneck to growth—they simply can't do it all at a larger scale. So they make key hires to replace themselves in selected functions—for example, a technical founder hires a head of sales and delegates authority to find, sell, and close new accounts. At the same time, founders usually find it challenging to determine how much authority to give up (too much and the business could get ruined; too little and they'll get burned out trying to manage it all).

As the business and surrounding context develop over time, people settle into their roles and ways of operating. The structure seems to happen organically. From an outsider's perspective, it may be hard to figure out how and why the company looks and acts the way it does. And yet, from the inside, we grow used to things over time and question them less: "It's just how we do things around here." Organizations continue to operate, business as usual, until a new opportunity or a market crisis strikes and they realize they can't succeed with their current structures any more.

What are the signs that a structure isn't working? You'll know it's time to change things when inertia seems to dominate—in other words, the strategy and opportunity seem clear and people have bought in, yet the company can't achieve escape velocity. Perhaps it's repeating the same execution mistakes or making new hires that repeatedly fail (often a sign of structural imbalance rather than bad hiring decisions). There may be confusion among functions and roles, decision-making bottlenecks within the power centers, or simply slow execution all around. If any of these things are happening, it's time to do the hard but rewarding work of creating a new structure.

Here are five rules of organizational structure, along with the most common mistakes that companies make by not following them. As you read on, see if your organization has made any of them. If so, it's a sure sign that your current structure is having a negative impact on performance.

Rule #1: When the Strategy Changes, Change the Structure

Every time the strategy changes—including when there's a shift to a new stage of the execution lifecycle—you'll need to re-evaluate and change the structure. The classic mistake made in restructuring is that the new form of the organization follows the old one to a large degree. That is, a new strategy is created but the old hierarchy remains embedded in the so-called "new" structure. Instead, you need to make a clean break with the past and design the new structure with a fresh eye. Does that sound difficult? It generally does. The fact is that changing structure in a business can seem really daunting because of all the precedents that exist—interpersonal relationships, expectations, roles, career trajectories, and functions. And in general, people will fight any change that results in a real or perceived loss of power. All of these things can make it difficult to make a clean break from the past and take a fresh look at how the business should be now. There's an old adage that you can't see the picture when you're standing in it. It's true. It also means that when restructuring, you need to help your staff look at things with fresh eyes. For this reason, restructuring done wrong will exacerbate attachment to the status quo and natural resistance to change. Restructuring done right, on the other hand, will address and release resistance to structural change, helping those affected to see the full picture as well as to understand and appreciate their new roles in it.

Rule #2: Don't Allow Functions Focused on Efficiency to Control Functions Focused on Effectiveness

Efficiency will always tend to overpower effectiveness. Because of this, you'll never want to have functions focused on effectiveness (sales, marketing, people development, account management, and strategy) reporting to functions focused on efficiency (operations, quality control, administration, and customer service). For example, imagine a company predominantly focused on achieving Six Sigma efficiency (doing things "right"). Over time, the processes and systems become so efficient and tightly controlled, that there is very little flexibility or margin for error. By its nature, effectiveness (doing the right thing), which includes innovation and adaptation to change, requires flexibility and margin for error. Keep in mind, therefore, that things can become so efficient that they lose their effectiveness. The takeaway here is: Always avoid having functions focused on effectiveness reporting to functions focused on efficiency. If you do, your company will lose its effectiveness over time and it will fail.

Rules #3: Don't Allow Functions Focused on Short-Range Results to Control Functions Focused on Long-Range Development

Just as efficiency overpowers effectiveness, the demands of today always overpower the needs of tomorrow. That's why the pressure you feel to do the daily work keeps you from spending as much time with your family as you'd like. It's why the pressure to hit this quarter's numbers makes it so hard to maintain your exercise regime. And it's why you never want to have functions that are focused on long-range development (branding, strategy, R&D, people development, etc.) reporting to functions focused on driving daily results (sales, running current marketing campaigns, administration, operations, etc.). For example, what happens if the marketing strategy function (a long-range orientation focused on branding, positioning, strategy, etc.) reports into the sales function (a short-range orientation focused on executing results now)? It's easy to see that the marketing strategy function will quickly succumb to the pressure of sales and become a sales support function. Sales may get what it thinks it needs in the short run but the company will totally lose its ability to develop its products, brands, and strategy over the long range as a result.

Rule #4: Balance the Need for Autonomy with the Need for Control

There is an inherent and natural conflict between autonomy and control. One requires freedom to produce results, the other needs to regulate for greater efficiencies. The design principle here is that as much autonomy as possible should be given to those closest to the customer (functions like sales and account management) while the ability to control for systemic risk (functions like accounting, legal, and HR) should be as centralized as possible. In addition, the autonomy to sell and meet customer needs should always take precedence in the structure because without sales and repeat sales, the organization will quickly cease to exist. At the same time, the organization must exercise certain controls to protect itself from systemic harm (the kind of harm that can destroy the entire organization).

Rather than trying to make these functions play nice together, this design principle stems from a recognition of their inherent conflict, plans for it, and creates a structure that attempts to harness it for the overall good of the organization. For example, if Sales is forced to follow a bunch of bureaucratic accounting and legal procedures to win a new account, sales will suffer. However, if the sales team sells to a bunch of under-qualified leads that can't pay, the whole company suffers. Therefore, Sales should be able to sell without restriction but also bear the burden of underperforming accounts. At the same time, Accounting and Legal should be centralized because if there's a loss of cash or a legal liability, the whole business is at risk. So the structure must call this inherent conflict out and make it constructive for the entire business.

Rule #5: Put the Right People in the Right Functions

I'm going to talk about how to avoid this mistake in greater detail shortly but the basics are simple to grasp. Your structure is only as good as the people operating within it and how well they're matched to their jobs. Every function has a group of activities it must perform. At their core, these activities can be understood as expressing PSIU requirements. Every person has a natural PSIU style. It's self-evident that when there's close alignment between job requirements and an individual's style and experience then they'll perform at a higher level.

In the race for market share, however, companies make the mistake of mismatching styles to functions because of perceived time and resource constraints. For example, imagine a company that just lost its VP of sales who is a PsIu (Producer/Innovator) style. They also have an existing top-notch account manager who has a pSiU (Stabilizer/Unifier) style. Because management believes they can't afford to take the time and risk of hiring a new VP of sales, they move the account manager into the VP of sales role and give him a commission-based sales plan in the hope that this will incentivize him to perform as a sales person. Will the account manager be successful? No. It's not in his nature to hunt new sales. It's his nature to harvest accounts, follow a process, and help customers feel happy with their experience. As a result, sales will suffer and the account manager, once happy in his job, is now suffering too. While we all have to play the hand we're dealt with, placing people in misaligned roles is always a recipe for failure. If you have to play this card, make it clear to everyone that it's only for the short run and the top priority is to find a candidate who is the right fit as soon as possible.

Structure Done Wrong: An Example to Avoid

Below is a picture of a typical business structure done wrong. The company is a software as a service (SaaS) provider that has developed a new virtual trade show platform. They have about ten staff and $2M in annual revenues. I received this proposed structure just as the company was raising capital and hiring staff to scale its business and attack multiple industry verticals at once. In addition to securing growth capital, the company's greatest challenge is shifting from a startup in which the two co-founders do almost everything to a scalable company where the co-founders can focus on what they do best.

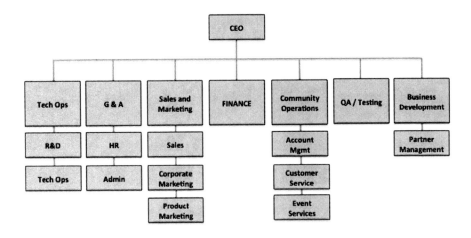

Figure 44. Structure done wrong. Can you tell what's wrong with this picture?

So what's wrong with this structure? Several things. First, this proposed structure was created based on past precedents within the company, not the core functions that need to be performed in order to execute the new strategy. This will make for fuzzy accountability, an inability to scale easily, new hires struggling to make a difference and navigate the organization, and the existing team having a hard time growing out of their former hats into dedicated roles. It's difficult to tell what key staff the company should hire and in what sequence. It's more likely that current staff will inherit functions that they've always done or that no one else has been trained to do. If this structure is adopted, the company will plod along, entropy and internal friction will rise, and the company will fail to scale.

The second issue with the proposed structure is that efficiency functions (tech ops and community operations) are given authority over effectiveness functions (R&D and account management). What will happen in this case? The company's operations will become very efficient but will lose effectiveness. Imagine being in charge of R&D, which requires exploration and risk taking, but having to report every day to tech ops, which requires great control and risk mitigation. R&D will never flourish in this environment. Or imagine being in charge of the company's key accounts as the account manager. To be effective, you must give these key accounts extra care and attention. But within this structure there's an increasing demand to standardize towards greater efficiency because that's what community operations requires. Because efficiency always trumps effectiveness over time, this structure will cause the company to lose its effectiveness.

Third, short-run functions are given authority over long-run needs. For example, Sales and Marketing are both focused on effectiveness but should rarely, if ever, be the same function. Sales has a short-run focus, Marketing a long-run focus. If Marketing reports to Sales, then Marketing will begin to look like a sales support function, instead of a long-run positioning, strategy, and differentiation function. As market needs shift, the company's marketing effectiveness will lose step and focus. It won't be able to meet the long-run needs of the company.

Fourth, it's impossible to distinguish where the authority to meet customer needs resides and how the company is controlling for systemic risk. As you look again at the proposed structure, how does the company scale? Where is new staff added and why? What's the right sequence to add them? Who is ultimately responsible for profit and loss? Certainly it's the CEO but if the CEO is running the day-to-day P&L across multiple verticals, then he is not going to be able to focus on the big picture and overall execution. At the same time, who is responsible for mitigating systemic risk? Within this current structure, it's very likely that the CEO will never extract himself from those activities he's always done and yet shouldn't still be doing if the business is going to scale. If he does attempt to extract himself from them, he will delegate without the requisite controls in place and the company will make a major mistake that threatens its life.

Structure Done Right

Below is a picture of how I realigned the company's structure to match its desired strategy. Here are some of the key things to recognize about this new structure and why it's superior to the old one. Each box represents a key function that must be performed by the business in its chosen strategy. Again, this is not an org chart. One function may have multiple people such as three customer service reps within it and certain staff may be wearing multiple hats. So when creating the structure, ignore the people involved and just identify the core business functions that must be performed. Again, first we want to create the right structure to support the chosen strategy. Then we can add roles and hats.

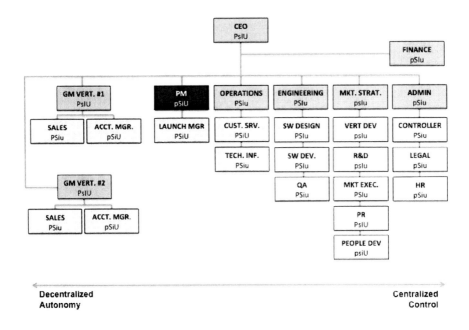

Figure 45. Structure done right. Can you tell how to scale this company?

How to Read this Structure

At the bottom of the structure you'll see an arrow with "decentralized autonomy" on the left and "centralized control" on the right. That is, your goal is to push decision-making and autonomy out as far as possible to the left of the structure for those functions closest to the customer. At the same time you need to control for systemic risk on the right of the structure for those functions closest to the enterprise. There is a natural conflict that exists between decentralized autonomy and centralized control. This structure recognizes that conflict, plans for it, and creates a design that will harness and make it constructive. Here's how.

Within each function, you'll see a label that describes what it does, such as "CEO," "Sales," or "Engineering." These descriptions are not work titles for people but basic definitions of what each function does. Next to each description is its primary set of PSIU forces. PSIU is like management shorthand that describes the forces of each function. For example, the CEO function needs to produce results, innovate for changing demands, and keep the team unified: PsIU.

Identifying the PSIU code for each function is helpful for two reasons. One, it allows a shared understanding of what's really required to perform a function. Two, when it's time to place people into hats and roles within those functions, it enables you to find a match between an individual's management style and the requirements for the role itself. For example, the account management function requires following a process and displaying a great aptitude towards interaction with people (pSiU). Intuitively, you already know that you'd want to fill that role with a person who naturally expresses a pSiU style. As I mentioned earlier, it would be a mistake to take a pSiU account manager and place them into a sales role that requires PSiu, give them a commission plan, and expect them to be successful. It's against their very nature to be high driving—and no commission plan is going to change that. It's always better to match an individual's style to a role, rather than the other way around.

Now that you understand the basics of this structure, let's dive into the major functions so you can see why I designed it the way I did. You may want to refer back to

Figure 45 to visualize where each function was placed on the map.

The General Manager (GM) Function

The first and most important thing to recognize is that, with this new structure, it's now clear how to scale the business. The green boxes "GM Vertical #1 and #2" on the far left of the structure are called business units. The business units represent where revenues will flow into the organization. They're colored green because that's where the money flows. The GM role is created either as a dedicated role or in the interim as a hat worn by the CEO until a dedicated role can be hired. Each business unit recognizes revenue from the clients within their respective vertical. How the verticals are segmented will be determined by business and market needs and the strategy. For example, one GM may have authority for North America and the other for Asia/Pacific. Or one might have authority for the entertainment industry and the other for the finance industry. Whatever verticals are chosen, the structure identifies authority and responsibility for them. Notice that the code for the GM/PsIU is identical to the CEO/PsIU. This is because the GMs are effectively CEOs of their own business units or can be thought of as future CEOs in training for the entire organization.

Underneath each green business unit is a Sales role, responsible for selling new accounts and an Account Management role, responsible for satisfying the needs of key clients. Essentially, by pushing the revenue-driving functions to the far left of the structure, we are able to decentralize autonomy by giving each GM the authority and responsibility to drive revenue, acquire new customers, and meet the needs of those customers. Each GM will have targets for revenue, number of customers, and client satisfaction. They will also have a budget and bonus structure.

The Product Manager (PM) Function

To the immediate right of the green business units is a black box called "PM" or Product Manager. The function of the Product Manager is to manage the competing demands of the different verticals (the green boxes to its left) as well as the competing demands of the other business functions (the grey boxes to its right) while ensuring high product quality and market fit and driving a profit. The grey boxes to the right of the Product Manager—CEO, Finance, Operations, Engineering, Marketing Strategy, and Admin—represent the rest of the core organizational functions. Effectively, these functions provide services to the green business units so that those units have products to sell to their markets. The revenue that the business generates pays for those internal services. Profits are derived by subtracting the cost of those services from the revenues generated by the business units. A Launch Manager who helps to coordinate new product releases among the business units supports the Product Manager.

The code for the Product Manager is pSiU. That is, we need the Product Manager to be able to stabilize and unify all of the competing demands from the organization. What kind of competing demands? The list is almost endless. First, there will be competing demands from the verticals. One vertical will want widget X because it meets the needs of their customers; the other will want widget Z for the same reasons (and remember that this particular company's strategy is to run multiple verticals off a single horizontal platform). Operations will want a stable product that doesn't crash and integrates well within the existing infrastructure. Engineering will want a cutting-edge product that displays innovative features. Marketing Strategy will want a product that matches the company's long-range plans. Administration will want a product that doesn't cause the company to get sued. The CEO will want a product that tells a great story to the marketplace. Finance will want a product that generates significant ROI or one that doesn't require a lot of investment, depending on its lifecycle stage. So the list of inherent conflicts runs deep.

The reason we don't want a psIu in the Product Manager is that at this stage of the company's lifecycle, the innovative force is very strong within the founding team, which will continue to provide that vision and innovation in another role, new Vertical Development and R&D under Marketing Strategy (more on this later). Nor do we want a Psiu in the Product Manager function because a big producer will focus on driving forward quickly and relentlessly (essential in the earlier stages of the product lifecycle) but will miss many of the details and planning involved with a professional product release (essential at this stage of the product lifecycle).

It's worth discussing why we want the product P&L to accrue to the Product Manager function and not the CEO or GMs. By using this structure, the CEO delegates autonomy to the GMs to drive revenue for their respective verticals and for the Product Manager to drive profits across all verticals. Why not give P&L responsibility to the CEO? Of course, the ultimate P&L will roll up to the CEO but it's first recognized and allocated to the Product Manager. This allows the CEO to delegate responsibility for product execution in the short run while also balancing the long-range needs of the product and strategy.

We don't give the Product Manager function to the GMs at this stage for a different reason. If we did, the product would have an extreme short-run focus and wouldn't account for long-run needs. The business couldn't adapt for change and it would miss new market opportunities. At the same time, the GMs need to have significant input into the product features and functions. That's why the Product Manager is placed next to the GMs and given quite a lot of autonomy—if the product isn't producing results in the short run for the GMs, it's not going to be around in the long run. At the same time, the product must also balance and prioritize long-range needs and strategy and that's why it doesn't report to the GMs directly.

If the business continues to grow, then one of the GMs will become the head of an entire division. Think of a division as a grouping of multiple similar verticals. In this case, the Product Manager function may in fact be placed under the newly formed division head because it is now its own unique business with enough stability and growth to warrant that level of autonomy. Remember that structures aren't stagnant and they must change at each new stage of the lifecycle or each change in strategy. For this current stage of the lifecycle, creating a dynamic tension between the GMs, the Product Manager, and the rest of the organization is highly desired because it will help to ensure a sound product/market/execution fit.

The Operations Function

To the immediate right of the Product Manager is Operations. This is the common services architecture that all GMs use to run their business. It is designed for scalable efficiency and includes such functions as Customer Service and Technology Infrastructure. Notice how all of these functions are geared towards short-run efficiency, while the business still wants to encourage short-term effectiveness (getting new clients quickly, adapting to changing requests from the GMs, etc.) within these roles and so it gives more autonomy to this unit than to those to the right of it. The code for Operations is PSiU because we need it to produce results for clients every day (P). It must be highly stable and secure (S) and it must maintain a client-centric perspective (U). It's important to recognize that every function in the business has a client whom it serves. In the case of Operations, the clients are both internal (the other business functions) and external (the customers).

The Engineering Function

Going from left to right, the next core function is Engineering. Here the core functions of the business include producing effective and efficient architectures and designs that Operations will use to do their work, such as SW Design, SW Development, and QA. Notice, however, that the deployment of new software is ultimately controlled by the Product Manager (Launch Manager), which provides an additional QA check on software from a business (not just a technology) perspective. Like Operations, Engineering is also short-run oriented and needs to be both effective and efficient. It is given less relative autonomy in what it produces and how it produces it due to the fact that Engineering must meet the needs of all other business functions, short- and long-run. The code for Engineering is PSIu because we need it to produce results now (P); to have quality code, architecture, and designs (S); and to be able to help create new innovations (I) in the product.

The Marketing Strategy Function

The next core function is Marketing Strategy. Marketing Strategy is the process of aligning core capabilities with growing opportunities. It creates long-run effectiveness. Its code is psIu because it's all about long-term innovation and nurturing and defending the vision. Sub-functions include new Vertical Development (early stage business development for future new verticals that will ultimately be spun out into a GM group), R&D, Marketing Execution (driving marketing tactics to support the strategy), PR, and People Development. A few of these sub-functions warrant a deeper explanation.

The reason new Vertical or Business Development is placed here is that the act of seeding a new potential vertical requires a tremendous amount of drive, patience, creativity, and innovation. If this function were placed under a GM, then it would be under too much pressure to hit short-run financial targets and the company would sacrifice what could be great long-term potential. Once the development has started and the vertical has early revenue and looks promising, it can be given to a new or existing GM to scale.

The purpose of placing R&D under Marketing Strategy is to allow for the long-run planning and innovative feature development that can be applied across all business units. The short-run product management function is performed by the Product Manager. The Product Manager's job is to manage the product for the short run while the visionary entrepreneur can still perform R&D for the long run. By keeping the Product Manager function outside of the GM role, New Product Development can more easily influence the product roadmap. Similarly, by keeping the Product Manager function outside of Marketing Strategy, the company doesn't lose sight of what's really required in the product today as needed by the GMs. Similarly, if the R&D function was placed under Engineering, it would succumb to the short-range time pressure of Engineering and simply become a new feature development program—not true, innovative R&D.

The reason Marketing Execution is not placed under the GM is that it would quickly become a sales support function. Clearly, the GM will want to own his or her marketing execution and s/he may even fight to get it. It's the CEO's role, however, to ensure that Marketing Execution supports the long-range strategy and therefore Marketing Execution should remain under Marketing Strategy.

The basis for placing People Development under Marketing Strategy rather than under HR is that People Development is a long-range effectiveness function. If it's placed under HR, then it will quickly devolve into a short-range tactical training function. For a similar reason, recruitment is kept here because a good recruiter will thrive under the long-range personal development function and will better reflect the organization's real culture.

The Finance and Admin Functions

To the far right of the organization are the Administrative functions. Here reside all of the short-run efficiency or Stabilizing functions that, if performed incorrectly, will quickly cause the organization to fail. These functions include Controller (AR/AP), Legal, and the HR function of hiring and firing. Notice, however, that the Finance function is not grouped with Admin. There are two types of Finance. One, cash collections and payments, is an Admin function. The other, how to deploy the cash and perform strategic financial operations, is a long-run effectiveness function. If Finance is placed over or under Admin, the company will suffer from lack of effectiveness or a lack of efficiency, respectively. Allowing one function to control cash collections and cash deployments also creates a tremendous liability risk. It's better to separate these functions for better performance and better control.

The CEO Function

The top function is the CEO. Here resides the ultimate authority and the responsibility to keep the organization efficient and effective in the short and long run. The code for the CEO is PsIU because this role requires driving results, innovating for market changes, and keeping the team unified. By using this structure, the CEO delegates autonomy to the GMs to produce results for their respective verticals. The GMs are empowered to produce results and also to face the consequences of not achieving them by "owning" the revenue streams. The CEO has delegated short-run Product Management to produce a profit according to the plan and simultaneously balances short- and long-run product development needs. At the same time, the CEO protects the organization from systemic harm by centralizing and controlling those things that pose a significant liability. So while the GMs can sell, they can't authorize contracts, hire or fire, or collect cash or make payments without the authorization of the far right of the structure. Nor can they set the strategy, destroy the brand, or cause a disruption in operations without the authority of the CEO and other business units.

The goal of structure is to create clarity of authority and responsibility for the core organizational functions that must be performed and to create a design that harnesses the natural conflict that exists between efficiency and effectiveness, short run and long run, decentralization and control. A good CEO will encourage the natural conflict to arise within the structure and then deal with it in a constructive way.

Remember that within any structure, individuals will play a role and, especially in a start-up environment, wear multiple hats. How you fill roles and hats is to first identify and align the core functions to support the organization's strategy. Then, assign individuals to those functions as either a role or a hat. In the particular structure I discussed here, the role of CEO was played by one founder who also wore the temporary hats of GM Vertical #1 and #2 until a new GM could be hired. The other founder played the role of both Product Manager and Engineer until the latter role could be hired. Clearly delineating these functions allowed them both to recognize which roles they needed to hire first so that they could give up the extra hats and focus on their dedicated roles to grow the business. Going forward, both founders will share a hat in Marketing Strategy, with one of them focused on new Business Development and the other on R&D. These Marketing Strategy hats play to the strength of each founder and allow them to maintain the more creative, agile aspects of entrepreneurship once the business structure is in place for day-to-day strategy execution.

How to Design Your Organization's Structure

The first step in designing the new structure is to identify the core functions that must be performed in support of the business strategy, what each function will have authority over and be accountable for, and how each function will be measured (Key Performance Indicators or KPIs). Then, following the five rules of structure above, place those functions in the right locations within the organizational structure. Once this is completed, the structure acts as a blueprint for an organizational chart that calls out individual roles and hats. A role is the primary task that an individual performs. A hat is a secondary role that an individual performs. Every individual in the organization should have one primary role and—depending on the size, complexity, and resources of the business—may wear multiple hats. For example, a startup founder plays the CEO role and also wears the hats of Business Development and Finance. As the company grows and acquires more resources, she will give up hats to new hires in order to better focus on her core role.

Getting an individual to gracefully let go of a role or hat that has outgrown them can be challenging. They may think, "I'm not giving up my job! I've worked here for five years and now I have to report to Johnny-Come-Lately?" That's a refrain that every growth-oriented company must deal with at some point. One thing that can help this transition is to focus not on the job titles but on the PSIU requirements of each function. Then you help the individual identify the characteristics of the job that they're really good at and enjoy and seek alignment with a job that has those requirements. For example, the title VP of sales is impressive. But if you break it down into its core PSIU requirements, you'll see that it's really about cold calling, managing a team, and hitting a quota (PSiU). With such a change in perspective, the current director of sales who is being asked to make a change may realize, "Hmm . . . I actually HATE cold calling and managing a team of reps. I'd much rather manage accounts that we've already closed and treat them great. I'm happy to give this up." Again, navigating these complex emotional issues is hard and can cost the company a lot of energy. This is one of the many reasons that using a sound organizational restructuring process is essential.

A structural diagram may look similar to an org chart but there are some important differences. An org chart shows the reporting functions between people. What we're primarily concerned with here, on the other hand, are the functions that need to be performed by the business and where authority will reside in the structure. The goal is to first design the structure to support the strategy (without including individual names) and then to align the right people within that structure. Consequently, an org chart should follow the structure, not the other way around. This will help everyone avoid the trap of past precedents that I discussed earlier. This means—literally—taking any individual name off the paper until the structure is designed correctly. Once this is accomplished, individual names are added into roles and hats within the structure.

After restructuring, the CEO works with each new functional head to roll out budgets, targets, and rewards for their departments. The most important aspect of bringing a structure to life, however, isn't the structure itself, but rather the process of decision making and implementation that goes along with it. The goal is not to create islands or fiefdoms but an integrated organization where all of the parts work well together. If structure is the bones or shape of an organization, then the process of decision making and implementation is the heart of it. I'm going to discuss this process in greater detail in the following chapter.

It can take a few weeks to a few months to get the structure humming and people comfortable in their new roles. You'll know you've done it right when the structure fades to the background again and becomes almost invisible. It's ironic that you do the hard work of restructuring so you can forget about structure. Post integration, people should be once again clear on their roles, hats, and accountabilities. The organization starts to really perform and execution speed picks up noticeably. Roaring down the tracks towards a common objective is one of the best feelings in business. A good structure makes it possible.

Lex Sisney

19. Aligning the Decision-Making and Implementation Process

E
arlier, I shared that every business has mass, which is a measure of its resistance to change. The challenge in getting an organization to change direction is the fact that its mass isn't neatly self-contained. Rather, it's scattered throughout its people, systems, structures, and processes—and the collective inertia causes resistance to change. In order to get the organization to execute on its strategy, you've got to get the mass contained and headed in one direction. I call this "gathering the mass."

Having aligned vision and values, as well as an aligned organizational structure, is the first step. This helps to hold the mass together and keep internal friction low. If you have misalignment in these areas, then no matter what, you're not going to get very far. Making the organization take action and move quickly in a chosen direction, however, requires that one thing be done well: the process of making and implementing decisions. Why? Because at the most fundamental level, a business is simply a decision-making and implementation system. Think about it—every problem and opportunity require a decision to be made (deciding to do nothing is a decision too) and a solution to be implemented. If the business does this well—if it continually makes good decisions and implements them fast—then its momentum will increase and it can be very successful.

What's ironic about the process of decision making and implementation is that most businesses don't even think of it as a process (in case you're wondering, decision making and implementation are not two distinct things. They're really two parts of one process that must go hand in hand). While there's usually a recognized process for functions like Sales and Customer Service, the process for decision making and implementation is often operating haphazardly. Like many of the principles I discuss in my work, however, it's a crucial *meta-level* process with important applications all across the board.

In order to help your business accelerate its execution speed, I'm going to explain what an effective decision-making and implementation process is, how to do it well, who should be involved, and when to use it.

The Rhythm of Decision Making and Implementation

There's a rhythm to decision making and implementation and most organizations screw it up. The right rhythm is slow-quick. It's not quick-slow or quick-quick—and it's clearly not slow-slow. What do I mean? Slow-quick means that you spend adequate time in making a good decision and then fly like a rocket on implementation. Don't do the opposite. In other words, don't make half-baked rapid-fire decisions that get bogged down on implementation. Don't be that company that confuses rapid decision making with rapid implementation. Also, don't be that company that's just bogged down and lethargic generally. There's a rhythm to life, a rhythm to dance, and a rhythm to decision making and implementation. Be astute and aware enough to know which rhythm to activate and when.

The most common reason companies get this rhythm wrong is time pressure. You need to be able to suspend time pressure in the decision-making phase of the process and then use it to your advantage during the implementation phase. Allow me to explain. Constant time pressure results in poor decisions. When a company's leadership feels a tremendous amount of pressure to execute quickly in a nebulous environment—and there's a feeling that doing something is better than doing nothing—it will tend to make half-baked, rapid-fire decisions. This approach is a classic folly because the team fails to see the complete picture before them. Under time pressure, it fails to take into account different perspectives, gather enough information, get buy-in, find new insights in the data, make a well-rounded decision, and reinforce that decision. The result is a poor decision that gets bogged down on implementation. The team tries to go quick-quick but the result is quick-slow.

If you've ever worked in a "fire-ready-aim" setting, then you already know that making rapid-fire decisions doesn't result in faster execution speed—which you do want. What happens instead is that a lot of decisions get rattled off, pile up, and create bottlenecks on implementation. And unlike decision making, implementation is where you want to use time pressure to your advantage, setting clear outcomes and delivery dates. In other words, it's not about how fast you're deciding; it's about how fast you're implementing on a well-formed solution.

Many startup founders will change their strategy from one moment to the next, justifying this with something like, "We have to be nimble around here. The market is always shifting and we're trying to find our footing. We need to fail fast and keep trying. If you can't keep up, get off the boat." This is a perfect example of how the concept "fail fast" is often misunderstood. "Fail fast" is an expression used in high-tech startups. It means that, in environments with rapid change and time pressure, you can only find answers in the real world, not on a white board. You therefore want to get the product released promptly and tested in the hands of actual customers because this allows you to better understand their needs. If the product "fails," this is seen as net positive (assuming client expectations are managed) because it eliminates more uncertainty about what doesn't work and you can test again based on better information. However, "fail fast" isn't a creed you use to keep making poor, ill-formed decisions time and again. It means that you need to implement a good decision fast. In other words, it's a slogan for swift implementation, not erratic decision making.

Of course it's not only startups that suffer from fast decision making and poor implementation. A recent prominent example is NetFlix. In 2011, NetFlix announced that it would segment its business into two distinct brands, one focused on streaming (NetFlix) and the other on DVD delivery (Qwikster). In my opinion, Reed Hastings, the company CEO, was right to attempt to restructure the business into two distinct business units. In the company's quest to hurry a decision, however, they screwed up the implementation. They didn't set up a process to communicate and manage expectations with their customer base and key influencers; they didn't acquire the social media identifiers for Qwikster; and they didn't recognize that customers would balk at having two logins without a process to make it easy for them. The resulting market backlash really hurt them—cutting their market cap in half. Reed Hastings was later quoted as saying, "We simply moved too quickly, and that's where you get those missed execution details. It's causing, as you would expect, an internal reflectiveness. We know that we need to do better going forward. We need to take a few deep breaths and not move quite as quickly. But we also don't want to overcorrect and start moving stodgily."[12]

That's exactly right.

The truth is that fast execution requires a good decision-making process up front—and effective decision making takes time! It takes time to gather the right people, set the stage, gather data, generate insights, decide what to do, assign action items, and reinforce the decision. It's counterintuitive but the right path forward is to slow down on the decision making so that you can speed up on the implementation. In other words, you slow down to go fast.

Of course, this all presupposes that you actually have the time. If it's a real crisis, then you'll need to act swiftly and try to reduce the negative fallout later. But whatever you do, don't confuse acting swiftly with acting smartly.

---

[12] Nicola Kean, "Netflix Moved Too Fast, Hastings Admits." *Portfolio* (October 20, 2011). Retrieved from http://www.portfolio.com/views/blogs/pressed/2011/10/20/Netflix-CEO-Reed-Hastings-admits-they-moved-too-fast-on-Qwikster.

Getting the Right People in the Room

There's a really simple rule of thumb to remember for good decision making and fast implementation: *Identify who will be impacted by a decision downstream and involve them upstream in the decision-making process.* Intuitively, this makes sense. In your own life, would you prefer to decide what to do yourself or have someone tell you what to do? When you're given an opportunity to genuinely participate in a decision-making process, not only do you help to create a better decision through your unique insights, but you also become more willing to implement the decision itself. You feel a greater sense of ownership and less resistance to change.

Gathering a critical mass in the company—and specifically those who will be impacted downstream by a decision—also leads to better outcomes because different people see different pieces of the full picture. Each person impacted has a unique perspective on the problem or opportunity: One sees what to do (P); another has information on how to do it (S); another can see new ways to accomplish the same task (I); and yet another can empathize with how others will be impacted (U). Each person brings different information, experience, and knowledge to bear on the problem or opportunity, contributing to everyone seeing the full picture.

Here's a striking story of a CEO who failed to gather in the decision-making process upstream those who would be impacted downstream. I'm not sure where it originates but it's all over the web and I have to believe there's some truth to it because it sounds all too common. The story goes like this:

> A toothpaste factory had a problem: they sometimes shipped empty boxes, without the tube inside. This was due to the way the production line was set up, and people with experience in designing production lines will tell you how difficult it is to have everything happen with timings so precise that every single unit coming out of it is perfect 100% of the time. Small variations in the environment (which can't be controlled in a cost-effective fashion) mean you must have quality assurance checks smartly distributed across the line so that customers all the way down the supermarket don't get pissed off and buy someone else's product instead.
>
> Understanding how important that was, the CEO of the toothpaste factory got the top people in the company together and they decided to start a new project, in which they would hire an external engineering company to solve their empty boxes

problem, as their engineering department was already too stretched to take on any extra effort.

The project followed the usual process: budget and project sponsor allocated, RFP, third-parties selected, and six months (and $8 million) later they had a fantastic solution—on time, on budget, high-quality—and everyone in the project had a great time. They solved the problem by using some high-tech precision scales that would sound a bell and flash lights whenever a toothpaste box weighing less than it should. The line would stop, and someone had to walk over and yank the defective box out of it, pressing another button when done.

A while later, the CEO decides to have a look at the ROI of the project: amazing results! No empty boxes ever shipped out of the factory after the scales were put in place. Very few customer complaints, and they were gaining market share. "That's some money well spent!"—he says, before looking closely at the other statistics in the report.

It turns out that the number of defects picked up by the scales was 0 after three weeks of production use. It should've been picking up at least a dozen a day, so maybe there was something wrong with the report. He filed a bug against it, and after some investigation, the engineers come back saying the report was actually correct. The scales really weren't picking up any defects, because all boxes that got to that point in the conveyor belt were good.

Puzzled, the CEO travels down to the factory, and walks up to the part of the line where the precision scales were installed. A few feet before it, there was a $20 desk fan, blowing the empty boxes out of the belt and into a bin. "Oh, that—one of the guys put it there 'cause he was tired of walking over every time the bell rang," said one of the workers."

You wouldn't be reading this story if the CEO had taken the time to include the shop floor workers—those who would be most impacted by the decision—in the decision-making process itself. If he had, he likely would have saved six months and $7,999,980! But clearly it is neither time- nor cost-effective in most instances to gather every individual who will be impacted downstream in the decision-making process upstream. That's why a country uses a representative democracy, why a public company uses a board of directors, and also partly why parents are the legal guardians of their children. These gather the mass and centralize the decision making into one representative body. The same is true for your organization. It has a critical mass that can represent the rest of the company.

So who do you gather in? In order to effect change, you should gather only the minimum amount of critical mass into the decision-making process—and specifically, only those with authority, power, and influence over the implementation. Based on the notion of "CAPI" or "coalesced authority, power, and influence" developed by Ichak Adizes,[13] this principle powerfully explains the fundamental elements required for fast and effective implementation.

Authority

According to Ichak Adizes, authority is the legal right to decide "yes" and "no." Many people can say "no" in an organization but very few can actually say "yes." Think of authority like a crown and scepter. Whoever wears the crown has the authority to say "yes" and "no" within the context of what they want to achieve. In U.S. government, the President has authority to sign a bill into law or to veto it. That's a "yes" or a "no." In baseball, an umpire has authority to call balls and strikes. That's a "yes" or a "no" too. In a trial, the jury has the authority to decide guilt or innocence. Wherever you observe the ability to say "yes" and "no," that's authority.

To gather authority, you've got to get *at least* the lowest level of authority involved in the decision-making process. For example, imagine a director of operations who is charged with improving efficiency in a production line. There's a new machine that the director wants to purchase. If she goes and asks the VP of finance for the money, the VP of finance can say, "No, sorry, it's not in the budget" or "No, you need to get approval from the budget committee first." But notice how the VP of finance cannot also say, "Yes, here's your check" without additional authority being granted from somewhere else. Therefore, the VP of finance has no authority over this particular decision.

Don't confuse those who can say "yes" but not "no" with authority, either. In this case, the director brings the purchase request to a budgetary committee. The budgetary committee can only endorse items that are within the budget and that fit the budgetary guidelines. That is, if it's within the budget and fits the budgetary guidelines without any errors on the requisition, then the budgetary committee must say "yes." They have no authority to also say "no." If the director does get budgetary

---

[13] Ichak Adizes, *Managing Corporate Lifecycles* (Upper Saddle River, NJ: Prentice Hall, 1999).

committee approval, she may mistakenly believe that she's gotten authority for the project. She hasn't.

Instead, to gather authority, the director must seek out who can actually say "yes" *and* "no" to the purchase and involve him or her up front in the decision-making process. In this case, it may be herself (if the authority was granted to her by the CEO) or, if not, then it's probably the CEO. If she fails to do this, then she'll never have a clear indication of where the project really stands. If she's smart and if the decision is important, she'll involve the person with authority to say "yes" and "no" in the decision-making process itself.

Power

Power is the ability to help or hinder. Think of power like a lever whereby those who have power over implementation can effectively help lever things up or down. Power exists throughout the organization, not just at the top. For example, in the U.S. government, the President has authority but Congress has power. It can help or hinder the President's agenda. Even though you're a parent and have the authority to say "yes" or "no," your kids certainly have power in that they can help or hinder how you run the family. A CEO of a Fortune 500 company may seem to possess a lot of power (and actually does) but if you look closely, you'll see that the power also exists within the unions, customers, media, and management team—all of which can help or hinder the CEO's agenda.

To gather power, recognize who can help or hinder the implementation of your objective and involve them up front in the decision-making process. Returning to the previous example, who might help or hinder the director of operations' desire to improve efficiency? In addition to the director's boss, this would also include the staff who work on the production line, design the systems, and perform maintenance. Involving those with power up front will generally contribute to a better decision, which becomes their own. For example, it may be that a new machine isn't required to improve efficiency. Perhaps someone on the production line has a creative solution. If a new machine is required, however, those who will be responsible for using it can help to choose the right one based on their firsthand experience and won't resist it like they would if it was purchased and installed out of the blue. Asking those who will have to use a piece of equipment in their daily work for their opinion on features may seem blindingly obvious. But it's often overlooked as in the example of the toothpaste factory.

Influence

Influence is the ability to get what you want without relying on authority or power. Think of influence like a pulpit. Individuals with a great deal of influence rely on who they are, who they know, and what they say. For example, a politician on the campaign trail is attempting to gain votes through influence. A company launching a marketing campaign to impact brand awareness and buying behavior is also working through influence. When a salesperson is meeting with a prospect, they're also attempting to use influence to activate the prospect's authority to purchase.

To gather influence, you should recognize who has influence over the implementation and involve them up front in the decision-making process as well. Who can influence, positively or negatively, the director of operations' desire to improve efficiency and purchase a new machine? There's the influence of the boss and staff. There's also the influence of industry experts, case studies, and other buyers' testimonials. For example, if the director hires an industry consultant to assess the situation and make a recommendation, the consultant has influence over the outcome, but no authority or real power.

To drive this concept of gathering authority, power, and influence home, imagine that the circle below represents the size of the task that you want to accomplish. If it's a small task that you can do yourself, then you already have the authority, power, and influence coalesced and there's no need to involve anyone else. Just go do the task. But if this is a "big" task, this generally means that the mass of authority, power, and influence are spread out. There's a lot of mass that must first be coalesced into the decision-making process itself.

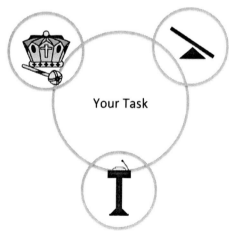

Figure 46. If your task is big, you'll need to gather the authority, power, and influence to make it happen.

If you don't gather in the mass, the resistance to change remains high, poor decisions get made because of a lack of vital input from those impacted by the decision, and implementation gets bogged down. Conversely, if you gather in the mass first, two things happen: (1) better decisions are made because they take into account multiple perspectives and interests and (2) implementation is swift because a critical mass of people within the organization have adopted the decision as their own (assuming a good decision-making process was followed, there's alignment in vision and values, and the structure is well designed) and they'll collectively drive it forward. To use a physics analogy, if you first coalesce the organizational mass, then you can "hit" it with a force of change and it will quickly accelerate in a new direction.

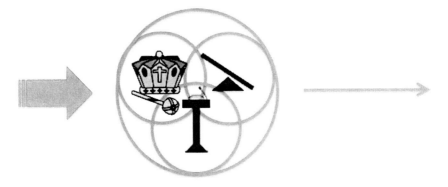

Figure 47. Once you've gathered in the authority, power, and influence, it's much easier to enact a change.

Now that you're familiar with the basic concepts of authority, power, and influence, you can see their effects everywhere you look. In a courtroom, the judge has power to decide what is admissible as evidence. The jurors have authority to decide a verdict. The lawyers rely on influence to sway the jury. Each side calls in witnesses who can help or hinder their case. In high-level selling, one of the first questions an experienced salesperson will ask is, "Who has authority to make a decision?" Then, if they're smart, they will do their best to get that person involved in the entire selling process. In other words, a great salesperson will always try to sell to the decision-maker directly. If there's a strong gatekeeper in the way, the salesperson must rely purely on influencing others who, in turn, will hopefully influence the final authority. Successful salespeople, therefore, usually have powerful networks of contacts (people who can help or hinder them in making introductions) and have mastered the art of influence to sway buyer behavior.

To gather authority, power, and influence literally means to get everyone in the same room (or at least on the same phone call) and to follow the six steps of effective decision making as a team. It does not involve periodically pinging the authority, power, and influence to update them on your progress. Nor does it involve informing them once a decision has been made. To reduce the resistance to change, you need to involve them in the decision-making process itself.

Why can't you periodically just ping the authority, power, and influence of your progress? For the same reason that lawyers do not conduct a jury trial independently and then report their findings for the jury to decide upon. A fair trial couldn't work this way. The coalesced authority, power, and influence must all participate in the decision-making process firsthand. Notice too that, if a jury member, lawyer, or judge can't be present, the trial is postponed. Similarly, if you can't get the authority, power, and influence in the room or on the phone at the same time, you would be well served to postpone the meeting to a later date. If you try to press ahead, you'll likely end up increasing the resistance to change, not decreasing it.

What Does an Effective Decision-Making and Implementation Process Look Like?

Before giving you the actual steps to effective decision making and implementation, I want to give you an immediate sense of what the process of making good decisions looks like by reminding you of a great scene from the 1990 film with Kevin Costner, *Dances with Wolves*. I call this scene the *"Dances with Wolves* Management Meeting" and there's a lot that modern-day management teams can learn from it. Unless you speak Sioux, you won't understand what they're saying—and it doesn't matter one bit. It is well known that 90 percent of communication is non-verbal anyway. The gist is that the senior tribe members have gathered to discuss what to do about foreigners invading their territory. You can compare that to any company faced with a cataclysmic market change and struggling with what to do about it.

Here's what I want to point out about this scene:

1. It's hard to figure out what to do and there's a lot of conflict. People in the circle have really strong opinions and they don't hold back in sharing them. At the same time, the conflict doesn't destroy the affinity that tribe members have for each another. They're debating the merits of different approaches in an attempt to find the best one. Each person has his say. When a person is

speaking, each member seems to be genuinely listening and considering that perspective.

2. The meeting has all the key influencers and centers of power in attendance. The chief and the tribe intuitively recognize that those impacted by the decision should be involved in the decision-making process. Why? When people fully participate in the decision-making process, they're less resistant to the implementation of its outcomes and often eagerly want to drive them forward. If the chief had skipped this meeting and decided what to do in isolation or with a few elders, the rest of the tribe would have resisted, questioned, doubted, and disagreed (e.g., "Why are we fighting?" or "Why are we fleeing?").

3. There is one decision maker. It's the wizened chief who sits back and listens until he's heard enough perspectives. He gives plenty of time for everyone to review the information and generate insights from it. Despite the fact that it's a critical decision, he doesn't get excited or agitated. He's calm; he's cool; he listens. Once that process is complete, he decides and people act. There's full debate pre-decision, no debate post-decision. Put another way, the meeting was fully participative but not democratic—there's one person ultimately in charge. Once the decision is made, it's time to stop debating and start executing.

4. The meeting doesn't linger. The tribe gathers together. They're all present and engaged. They invest as much time as they need and no more. Then they wrap. I'm willing to bet that most of your management meetings aren't run nearly as efficiently.

The Six Steps to an Effective Decision-Making and Implementation Process

The agile development methodology of the Agile Alliance provides us with a powerful and effective model for good decision making outlined in the six steps below:

Step 1—Set the Stage

Step 2—Gather Data

Step 3—Generate Insights

Step 4—Decide What to Do

Step 5—Assign Action Steps

Step 6—Reinforce

Step 1: Set the Stage

Once you've identified and gathered in the mass of authority, power, and influence, you need to set the stage of the decision-making process. Setting the stage means getting everyone in the room on the same page about why the meeting or project is taking place, the desired outcomes, the participants' roles and responsibilities (including who has authority to make the final yes/no decision), and the rules and expectations for the process. Because time pressure is the enemy of effective decision making, one of the most important things you can do when setting the stage is to create the right environment for the best decision to unfold. This requires unfreezing the group, getting initial buy-in to the problem/opportunity, and setting expectations on time management.

Unfreezing

One of the most important parts of setting the stage is easy to do but often skipped. It's what the founder of organizational psychology, Kurt Lewin, called "unfreezing."[14] What Lewin recognized in the early 1900s is that inertia exists within people just as it exists within objects. Basically, when you and I show up to a meeting, our bodies are present but our minds are not. Instead, we're stuck in mental inertia, still thinking about something else. The last phone call we were on. The emails we just received. A family or personal issue. We're hungry. Whatever. The list is infinite.

The only purpose of having a meeting is to have the team participate through the process as one unit, through which each participant brings their whole being, experience, knowledge, and awareness to the task at hand. This requires everyone involved to first unlock or unfreeze their mental inertia—in other words, to create a sense of space or mental capacity to focus on the task at hand and embody a future change.

It's actually pretty easy to unfreeze a group as long as you take a few minutes to do it. The simplest way is to get each participant to talk out loud. Just say something. Anything. It could be as simple as "How was your weekend?" or "What is costing your energy right now?" or "Ready?" What you'll notice is that it doesn't matter so much what the question is but rather that each participant simply say something out loud. For example, I

---

[14] Kurt Lewin, "Frontiers in Group Dynamics," in Dorwin Cartwright (ed.), *Field Theory in Social Science: Selected Theoretical Papers by Kurt Lewin* (Westport: Greenwood Press, 1951).

was facilitating a workshop this week and, after the group returned from a short break, I asked each person in turn, "Are you ready to continue?" One participant responded, "No, I'm not. I just got a really bad phone call about a deal I was trying to close. I'm devastated." He sat there for a few more moments; then he said, "OK, now that I cleared that out loud, I'm ready to go." Speaking out loud will always help to shift energy in a person and bring more presence to the task at hand.

Getting Initial Buy-in to the Problem or Opportunity

In addition to unfreezing the group, you'll want to help set the stage by ensuring that the group has a unified vision of what it's trying to accomplish. I recommend that you tie the desired outcomes for the team and/or project into the personal desired outcomes of the individual participants. One way to do this is to simply ask each person, "What is the desired outcome for this meeting (or this project) for you personally?" and write down his or her response. Then once each person has had a chance to state his or her desired outcomes, make sure that all the desired outcomes are aligned and attainable and, if not, address them up front accordingly. "This one seems out of scope for this particular project. What do you guys think?" Once you've got alignment on desired outcomes, people should be clear and eager to dive into the process.

The reason I suggest that you ask participants about personal desired outcome is that, when we have a personal interest in something, we're much more engaged in attaining it. Often people show up to a meeting with no clear idea why they are there in the first place. By asking "what's in it for you?" you'll help them to reflect on and clarify any potential rewards. "Hmmm, you know, I'd like to learn more about how XYZ works." Or, "I'd like to be part of a kick-ass team that really produces results." If a person has no personal desired outcome related to this meeting and/or project, it's a sign that they probably shouldn't be in that meeting.

Setting Expectations on Time Management

When it comes to setting expectations on time management in the decision-making process, here are some guidelines. Most of the time spent in decision making is invested in steps 1 to 3 (Setting the Stage, Gathering Data, and Generating Insights).

Once this is accomplished, it's pretty straightforward to complete step 4 (Deciding What to Do) and step 5 (Assigning Action Steps for Implementation). A general rule of thumb is to invest 80 percent of the time in steps 1 through 3 and 20 percent of the time in steps 4 through 6. In an hour-long meeting, 42 minutes would be allocated to setting the stage, gathering facts, and generating insights and just 18 minutes to deciding what to do, assigning action steps, and integration. If you feel that 18 minutes is not enough time to decide what to do, assign action steps, and integrate, it's a clear indication that you'll need to schedule a longer meeting. But don't skimp on the first three steps. That's where most of your time investment should occur. If you do skimp, it will come back to bite you through poor decisions and flawed implementations.

My grandfather used to say that the mind can only handle what the seat can endure. Speaking as a person who has a hard time sitting for long periods, I concur. My favorite way to handle this is to run 75-minute team sessions with a five to 15 minute break in between. This allows enough time for the group to make meaningful progress. At the same time, it allows the group enough space and personal freedom to restore the body, check email, make phone calls, etc. Get agreement from the group up front about the timeframes in which you'll run sessions and breaks. This will allow participants to focus on the task at hand.

A couple words of advice: There will be occasions when you need to spend more time in one part of the process than you were anticipating. If you are not able to complete your work in the allocated timeframe, you need to set a new meeting to continue where you left off. But remain disciplined around the timeframe of a given meeting. When it's time to break, break. When it's time to wrap, wrap. Also, make sure to unfreeze the group when they come back from a break or start a new session. The team needs to proceed through the process as one unit.

Step 2: Gather Data

Gathering the data means collecting all the available quantitative and qualitative facts related to the issue at hand from those present in the room. It's important to go through this process before speculating about causes, effects, and possible solutions. If you don't gather the facts, the group is going to lack a shared data set, miss the full picture, and make a half-baked decision. Each person will see the problem in a different light and no agreement will be reached on what the core issue really is.

Here's an example to show what happens when you skip gathering data. Imagine a technology company that is experiencing a 10 percent reduction from the previous quarter's sales. Alarmed, the board of directors asks the CEO to identify the problem and present a solution at the next board meeting. The CEO gathers the VP of sales, the VP of marketing, the CTO, and the CFO in a conference room and says, "All right. We're down 10 percent this quarter. The board wants answers. What are your solutions?" This approach to problem solving is a disaster in the making. Why? Because the leader skipped gathering data as a group and therefore missed the opportunity to create a shared data set and, from there, consolidating and reconciling the different perspectives on the issue.

In this scenario, the VP of sales, who's a hard-charging, task-focused type (Psiu) will likely point the finger at marketing: "We're not selling because we're not driving enough inbound leads. Get me more leads and we'll sell 'em!" The VP of marketing, who's more of a creative, big-picture type (psIu), will point the finger at technology: "We're not selling because the product features we've been requesting are six months behind schedule!" The CTO, who likes to keep things nice and stable (pSiu), will point the finger back at marketing and sales: "We're not selling because the business side keeps changing requirements in the middle of our production cycle!" And the CFO, who prefers to keep drama low (psiU), will respond with, "We're not selling because there's too much infighting!" After an hour of fruitless discussion, the CEO throws up his arms in exasperation, makes a rushed set of decisions, and barks out his orders to the team. Can you anticipate the outcome of this meeting?

What should have happened? The group should have first gathered data on multiple aspects of the problem. For example, what is the economic growth rate during that quarter? What are competitive sales figures? What is the client satisfaction rating? What facts do sales, marketing, technology, and finance have that can add clarity to the picture? Stick to data gathering here. Don't dive into solutions yet, no matter what. When someone tries to go for the solution (and they will) stop them: "We'll get to solutions in a bit but first let's make sure that we have a full picture. Let's keep gathering information."

What should you do if you don't have the data you need? Go get it. Break the meeting. Assign action steps for people to come back with good, clean data as soon as possible. Set a new meeting to continue with the information the team needs to make a good decision.

There are two reasons that gathering good data from the team is so critical. The first is that good information is like a light in the darkness. Change constantly alters reality—and the faster the change, the harder it is to see what's happening and adapt to it. What was a good decision last year/month/week may no longer be a good decision now. People change, markets adapt, situations alter, and technologies disrupt and get disrupted. Good information makes it possible to manage all this because it allows you to better understand and respond to each of the phases you're moving through. It reveals what's really happening now and provides insights into what might happen next.

The second reason to gather data as a group is that each person brings a different data set to the table. Without a shared frame of reference each person is going to operate as if his or her perspective were the right one, thus missing key elements of the situation. If, however, the entire team can all agree that "yes, this is the data and we believe it's correct and comprehensive," that opens the door to new perspectives and a coherent understanding of the situation. Once you have that, you're ready to move to the next step.

Step 3: Generate Insights

Now that the team can agree on the facts, it's time to leverage the collective wisdom of the group to generate insights. What might be causing these facts to occur? What are the underlying causes and what are the symptoms? It's important to get all the perspectives on the table and stimulate an environment of curious exploration versus blame and finger pointing. In the previous example, one insight might be that there's poor coordination between development and customer requirements. Another might be that sales are down because the economy tanked. Initially, it doesn't matter which insights are correct, only that the group is collectively generating them based on a shared set of facts. After you've collected all the perspectives, the group should come up with a unified, agreed-upon narrative around the nature of the situation and its causes.

Step 4: Decide What To Do

It's now time to collect ideas about possible solutions from everyone in the group and afterward for the authority in the room to decide what to do. Good decision making is not a democratic process; it's a participative process. By creating an environment of authentic group participation, the person who has the ultimate authority over implementation must now make the decision. Because those with power and influence over the implementation have been given the opportunity to have their voice heard, they should stand behind the decision. It does not mean that the decision will make everyone happy, but it does mean that the team now needs to back whatever decision is made. After facilitating over 100 group decision-making processes, I have yet to witness the ultimate authority make a decision that is at odds with the group. It's not that the authority is afraid to make a hard decision; rather, it's that everyone involved has reached the right decision together. When this occurs, it's actually pretty easy and fast to move ahead towards implementation.

Step 5: Assign Action Steps

Now that a basic decision has been made, it's time to assign action steps and amp up the time pressure on the implementation. In simple terms, the group needs to identify what to do, who will do it, and by when. You're setting clear deliverables, clear dates, and unarguable accountability to execute on that decision. In this part of the process, there may be a slight give and take between the authority in the room and those charged with performing different aspects of the implementation. Arthur Authority asks, "Frank, when do you think you can complete the XYZ analysis?" Frank replies, "I need to do a little research and speak with Marge. I'll have it to you by next Friday." If this is amenable to Arthur's needs, the action item gets accepted and written down: "Frank to complete XYZ analysis by next Friday." If it's not amenable, then Frank and Arthur need to identify ways to change the task or speed the process. Because they've gone through the entire process together, both Frank and Arthur are fully aware of the broader implications, needs, and purpose of the action item. Consequently, there's usually really easy agreement and clarity on action items. And when in doubt, lean towards more time pressure than less.

Compare this to a scenario where Arthur and Frank don't go through the decision-making process together. In this scenario, Arthur has to get one-on-one time with Frank, explain the situation, and attempt to get Frank to change his schedule and priorities. It's not always easy to do—and it generally results in a poorer decision and a bogged-down implementation.

Step 6: Reinforce

Reinforcement is essential to a well-run decision-making process. In this final phase, the group reflects on and integrates the process they just experienced and the decisions reached. It's not a chance to complain, but rather to verbally lock in and commit to the implementation. A simple way to reinforce and close the meeting is to poll the group on their individual experiences during the process, as well as their views on how to improve it or how to support the implementation. The authority in the room is the last person to speak and then the meeting is closed. The end result is always better decisions and greater buy-in, as well as execution, on the implementation. If not, it's a clear indication that the requisite level of authority, power, and influence weren't in the room, that there was a breakdown in the process, or that there's a greater underlying misalignment at the level of vision and values or structure.

Executing on Short-Range Tasks vs. Long-Range Business Development

Just as there is a particular rhythm to follow for effective decision making and implementation, there's a particular rhythm for managing business needs between short-range execution and long-range business development. From the chapter on organizational structure, you've learned that short-run needs always overpower long-range ones. You therefore need to create an organizational process that allows for effective long-range planning and development combined with short-range execution.

The rhythm goes like this. One to two times per year, a company council, represented by the key functional heads and key team members throughout the organization (those 1s and 2s you want to groom for the long term), should gather together off site to set the long-range (one-to-three-year) strategy and to align the organizational structure to support that strategy. The goal of this strategic alignment session is to allow everyone to focus on long-run changes impacting the market and the business and to identify potential improvement areas within the business. It's important to do this long-range work off site to stimulate a new and broader perspective among the team. Once the long-range strategy is identified, shorter-range goals and outcomes are set, key performance indicators (KPIs) are identified, and budgets and rewards are established for each business function.

Armed with a common long-range strategy, clearly defined authority and accountability within the structure, and defined short-range goals, the core functional heads form into a leadership team led by the CEO that meets weekly or biweekly on site to review progress, make decisions, and execute the plan. These short-range tactics support the long-range development plan. This shared alignment and dialogue among the leadership team members allows everyone to stay on the same page, track and adjust performance, and keep the friction low. It should also reduce the total number of meetings conducted each week because, instead of scheduling ad hoc meetings, decisions are funneled into regular leadership team meetings where a good decision-making process is followed.

Watch for Signs of Deeper Problems

As you gather the authority, power, and influence over the implementation into the decision-making process, you will be well served to also recognize the signs of organizational misalignment or inertia. If there's significant misalignment within the organization's Execution Diamond (Vision and Values, Structure, and People), then your task will be very challenging indeed. Instead, your best course of action would be to gather in the authority, power, and influence to first realign the Execution Diamond. Once that is aligned, you can then attack the problem or opportunity you want to resolve.

Lex Sisney

20. Aligning People for High Performance

I received a call the other day from a high tech CEO looking for advice. His company is seven years old, brings in about $10M in revenue, and serves a very narrow niche in silicon wafer manufacturing. During the past year, his company pre-sold a new product concept to one of their largest customers. This new product is very innovative and promises to open up a brand new market and transform the company into a $100M-a-year business in three years. The product is due for its beta implementation in six months and you can imagine that the CEO has a lot riding on the outcome.

The reason for his call was that he was feeling a lot of anxiety and frustration because his employees didn't seem to "get it." They weren't working hard enough, didn't seem truly motivated, took long lunch breaks, went home early, and were making bone-headed mistakes—mistakes that the CEO, who is very technically savvy, would have to constantly step in and fix. "What should I do?" he asked me. "What will motivate them to perform faster, better, and smarter? Should I offer more stock options and cash bonuses? Or fire some people and set an example?" "No," I told him, "None of those things are going to really solve your problem. If you want higher performance, the solution is to quit trying to motivate your employees and instead, create a setting that taps into their intrinsic motivations."

The Myth of Motivation

There's absolutely nothing you can do to motivate others. People are already intrinsically motivated, engaged, and interested. In fact, when you try to motivate people by offering incentives, threats, bribes, and rewards, you're actually creating a disincentive to work, lowering both job satisfaction and productivity.

If you doubt that people are naturally motivated, or perhaps you're thinking of someone who doesn't appear to be engaged, creative, or interested at all, I challenge you to look a little deeper. When you do, you'll see that everyone is highly engaged, motivated, and proficient at *something*. Here's one small example. I have a friend whose ten-year-old son is really struggling in school. He's a sweet kid but at school he acts listless and disinterested and seems unable to keep up with his homework. Last year, the school principal called in his parents and explained that their son was going to be asked to leave the school unless some drastic changes took place. Based on the school counselors' recommendation, the parents put the child on medication, got him into therapy, hired a tutor, and created a series of incentives and punishments around his school work. So far, the boy has made some progress and he's been able to remain in school. But my friend confesses that it's a constant struggle to have him stay on top of his homework, adjust his medication, keep him motivated, and generally help him thrive. It's clear that managing the situation has a tremendous cost for the entire family.

I really feel for my friend. The situation sounds stressful and exhausting on multiple levels. I imagine many organizational managers struggle in a similar way trying to get some of their employees to really "get it" and "get on board with the program." When I heard this story, I asked, "OK, so what is your son interested in? Where does he naturally put his energy and attention?" My friend's reply was telling: "Oh yeah, it's video games. He's super interested and passionate about playing his XBox. He studies and reads about the games constantly. He always wants to talk about them and play online with his friends. We have to limit his playing time and it's a constant fight between us."

I tried to point out the contradiction: "So, when it comes to his school work, your son is listless and unmotivated. When it comes to mastering his video games, he's incredibly passionate and self-directed in his pursuit of mastering video games. It doesn't seem that your son lacks motivation. On the contrary, he's highly motivated, studious, proficient, and shows an extreme amount of skill development. If his school work was designed like a video game, he could be getting straight A's. Your son isn't suffering from a lack of motivation. He's suffering from a current school setting that doesn't align with his skills, motivation, and interests. If you were able to change the setting, such as exposing him to a different school or different curriculum, you'd realize that your son has plenty of motivation, determination, and drive to succeed."

In this scenario, the parents, the counselors, and the school are missing out on the critical difference between motivation and setting. The boy doesn't need drugs and discipline to be motivated. He's already extremely motivated, just not around the things his parents and teachers want him to focus on. The same thing is true for your employees. Each person in your company is interested, self-directed, and self-motivated by something. The real question is this: Are they naturally talented, motivated and interested in the things you want them to be? It's a subtle but profound difference.

Everyone Get in Your Genius Zone!

As I discussed in Chapter 2, each of us has a genius zone, or a range of interests and types of activities in which we excel that naturally add to our energy and joy and inspire us to further develop our capabilities. Our

PSIU styles are one way in which components of our genius zone manifest themselves. When our work is spent mostly within our genius zone, we are highly productive, happy, engaged, and self-motivated. When our work is misaligned with our genius zone, we're unhappy, stressed, and less productive. This is a good thing to keep in mind when you work with your staff. For example, if an employee excels at process-type work (pSiu), you should give them more assignments involving that (pSiu). If someone enjoys and is strong at interacting and empathizing with people (psiU), then try to give them opportunities to interact with customers (psiU). The point is, once you're aware of what someone truly likes and excels at, to the extent possible, align them with job functions that give them the opportunity to do just that.

If, however, there is a complete mismatch between an individual's genius zone and the work at hand, rather than fixing the problem with carrots or sticks, the best course is to find a better fit as soon as possible. In other words, if the demands of the job are diametrically opposite to what energizes that person and, if no other suitable roles are available, then it is best to help them find another role, either within or outside the organization. You'll be shocked at what happens when you align someone into a role that supports their genius zone. In fact, you may no longer even recognize them.

In 1860, in the frontier town of Point Pleasant, Ohio, there was questionable-looking store clerk in his early thirties. According to reports, he wore a grim expression and disheveled clothes and caused a lot of consternation among the local townspeople. First, there were rumors that he had served in the military but resigned under a dark cloud. Next, it was said, he tried farming but failed in spectacular fashion. Then he dabbled in real estate and failed again. Now, there he was in Point Pleasant, working in his father's leather goods store. To hear the townspeople tell it, he was a sorry excuse for a merchant. He couldn't sell and didn't know much at all about his father's wares. There were also rumors that he had a big problem with whiskey. Then, in 1861, something cataclysmic happened. The Civil War broke out. Without a penny to his name and with limited future prospects, this "failed" young man enlisted as a volunteer. Less than two years later, he was promoted to major general. Eventually, he became president of the United States. His name was Ulysses S. Grant.

What caused Ulysses S. Grant to transform from an impoverished failure into the winning general of the Civil War and then into the President of the United States? You guessed it. The Civil War. Once the Civil War broke out, the setting or surrounding conditions radically changed. With a change in setting, Grant was able to apply his innate motivation, skills, and talents and quickly rise up the ranks. Without that change in setting, we might have never known General Grant's capabilities. Notice, too, that no amount of incentives, bonus plans, job training programs, coaching, or motivational tactics would have made a meaningful difference in the life of General Grant the shopkeeper, for example. He likely would have remained a surly drunk frustrated with his life conditions and lack of opportunities.

So, yes, you can attempt to change or influence behavior by offering incentives, job training programs, coaching, and other motivational tactics. These all have their place and can be valuable. The truth, however, is that your employees will either thrive or fail due to the *setting* in which they work and how well they're matched to their respective roles and interests.

The right organizational setting is created by aligning three of the key elements we've been discussing in this part of the book—vision and values, organizational structure, and the decision-making and implementation process. These elements of the execution diamond should be your priority, even before focusing on the "people" component. If these three sub-systems of the organization are out of alignment, then it's going to be very challenging for even the most talented and ambitious employee to be successful. However, when you align them to create the right setting, and place people into their respective genius zones, then everyone involved can perform at a higher level. Your team of B players will begin to show up as A players because of the setting you create, not the HR tactics you deploy.

If this seems airy-fairy or out of the question in your current work setting, then I'd challenge you to look deeper still. Even if you run a toxic industrial factory farm surrounded by blood, suffering, and unhealthy employees or a sweatshop run on child labor at ten cents an hour (I'm going for the most dismal work environments I can imagine), you still have a choice to make. You can take the lowest common denominator and try to control, cajole, monitor, and "motivate" your staff (if this is your current approach, how's it really working for you anyway?) or you can align people into jobs that fit their natural strengths and interests. If you do the latter, then your job of "managing" shifts from babysitting, firefighting, and cat herding to identifying and aligning strengths, communicating clear expectations, and providing constructive feedback. From a manager's perspective, then, the real question is not how to motivate or incentivize employees to perform but rather, "where is the natural affinity and alignment between this person's style, capabilities, and interests and the work that needs to be done?" In the short term, it may not feel easy to align people's roles with their respective genius zones, but if you want self-motivated, creative, and high-performing people for the long run—and actually enjoy managing them—it's the only choice to make.

Don't make the mistake of thinking otherwise. You can't change the fundamental nature of your employees any more than a parent can change the fundamental nature of their children. Guide it? Yes. Influence it? Certainly. Change it? Not a chance.

What About Compensation?

You might be asking, "But what about compensation, bonuses, stock options, profit sharing, performance reviews, career paths, retention tactics, and all the other elements of modern human resources theory? Aren't these things critical in creating aligned and high-performing employees?" The answer is no, not really. It's obviously important to pay fair compensation, to treat people with respect and dignity, to provide constructive feedback, to share the rewards of success, and to help people find fulfillment through their work—and there are many tactics that a leader can choose that are appropriate to the time, place, and organizational culture. There's no one right answer. But don't confuse these actions with the fundamentals of creating the right organizational setting and aligning people into roles in which they naturally thrive. If you get and keep alignment between a person's role and their genius zone and PSIU style, they'll be naturally motivated, engaged, learning, and growing. The HR tactics can be kept very simple. If there's no alignment, on the other hand, then even the most compelling compensation plan isn't going to inspire high productivity for long.

If you still don't believe that compensation doesn't dictate performance, just take a look at organizational cultures in your local church, school, softball team, or volunteer organization. What you'll find is very hard-working, dedicated people who, even in the face of obstacles, are committed to their cause. The tragic thing is that most companies that are failing to reach their full potential actually do the opposite of what they should. They put their efforts into motivational tactics, hiring analysis, compensation plans, performance reviews, and the like but skip out on the most critical aspect of getting people to perform at a high level: matching them to their strengths. It's like putting the cart before the horse. Sure, you can do it, but it's not going to cause the cart to go anywhere.

21. The Misaligned Organization and What to Do About It

I f you're wise, you'll pay attention to the early signs of misalignment in your organization and take action immediately to address them. You'll recognize when it's time to realign the organization when it isn't executing as fast as it needs to. Symptoms may include:

The founder's trap—the company can't seem to scale beyond the founder, resulting in a bottleneck to growth and execution.

Incomplete priorities—the company can't say "no" to various opportunities and therefore isn't committed to a clear and purposeful strategy.

Amnesia—the company seems to have forgotten what it really is and why it's really in business.

Internal friction—the company takes too much energy and effort to make simple decisions and get work done.

Cash crunch—the company has sales but no profits.

Loss of innovation—the company no longer innovates but acquires growth by buying other companies.

Poor team performance—the team isn't stepping up to the size of the opportunity.

Aligning your organization isn't something you draw up in isolation and then announce to the team. This is because the greatest plan in the world is only as good as the team-wide commitment to implementing it. You'll need to follow all the steps of a sound decision-making and implementation process and involve those with authority, power, and influence in the alignment process itself. This usually amounts to you and your core leadership team (5 to 15 people on average) going through the process together. Here's the six-phase process I've found most effective in aligning organizations for improved performance. In my experience, depending on the size and complexity of the business, it takes anywhere from one to three months to complete phases 1 to 5 and double that time to fully integrate those changes in the culture and optimize performance in phase 6.

Phase 1: Aligning the Strategy

The main thing to keep in mind when it comes to aligning or realigning the organization is that, no matter how bad things may be in the current environment, the organization will still naturally resist any change. So your first step is always to unfreeze, unlock, or drain away any resistance to change. My favorite method for doing this is to get the leadership team off site for one and a half days and, as part of a strategy session, take a holistic view of the organization. We look at where it currently is on its strategic roadmap, as well as any sources of entropy (friction and potential improvement areas) impacting execution. With a shared recognition of what's really happening versus what should be happening, the leadership team gets on the same page and commits to finding solutions. The desired outcome from the strategy session is group clarity and commitment to the chosen growth strategy; shared recognition of three to five key burning balls or obstacles and an action plan to address them; greater appreciation for individual styles and perspectives among the team; and recognition of key issues affecting team performance and how to address them. Armed with this information, awareness, and buy-in, you're ready for phase 2.

Phase 2: Aligning the Organizational Structure

The purpose of this stage is to create leadership team recognition and buy-in for the right organizational design to support the chosen growth strategy. Like the stage before it, this stage is best conducted off site with the leadership team and, if done well, takes one day to complete. The desired outcome should be group recognition and buy-in for: (1) the role requirements and key performance indicators (KPIs) for each business function; (2) the individuals who will perform each role or hats; (3) the talent gaps in the structure; and (4) the new hire priority sequence. The result is a new organizational structure that best supports the company's growth strategy.

Phase 3: Aligning the Organizational Management Process

This part of the process doesn't need to be conducted off site. Instead, it's really a matter of taking the outcomes (the strategy, KPIs, and short-range and mid-range goals gathered from the prior two phases) and ensuring that the management team is executing towards them with little hindrance. This usually requires a period of time spent gathering the right metrics and making the data easy to collect and report on. It also requires spending some extra time with members of the leadership team to ensure they fully understand and are performing well in their new roles. At the same time, the goals for longer-range business development need to be managed and tracked through a separate process. Basically, there's one process to execute on short-range tasks (which is handled during weekly leadership team meetings) and one process to execute on long-range business development (which is handled by a company council). In other words, don't attempt to manage long-range goals in a short-range setting. The combined result is better team-wide decision making, an improved capacity to prioritize in the face of change, and more rapid implementations.

Phase 4: Aligning Budgets, Targets, and Rewards

Phase 4 really goes hand in hand with phase 3. Based on the new strategy, structure, and roles, you're working with the leadership team to identify the budget and annual, quarterly, and monthly financial and operational targets for the business. The result is greater clarity and incentives for the entire organization, as well as a methodology to track financial and operational performance.

Phase 5: Aligning the Vision, Values, and People

While the prior phases equip the senior leadership team for success, this phase integrates that groundwork throughout the rest of the organization. You accomplish this by collaborating with the leadership team to help cascade the strategy, vision, values, roles, and expectations down to the rest of the company. The desired outcome is a shared understanding of everyone's role in shaping the company's success, vision, and values. The result is a strong organizational culture that supports overall momentum and accomplishment.

Phase 6: Optimization

From here on, until it's time to realign the organization again, it's a matter of optimizing overall company performance. The not-so-ironic thing is that, because you've invested the time and energy in getting the alignment right, you don't have to optimize much at all. The ball starts rolling downhill under its own inertia. The outcome is a higher-performing, more resilient organization that executes powerfully on its chosen growth strategy.

Lex Sisney

Epilogue: World 2.0

Around the world, entrepreneurship is transforming calamity into opportunity. Billions of people formerly disconnected from "first-world" knowledge and prosperity are rapidly becoming integrated through technology, communications, manufacturing, and trade. Yet with growing global prosperity, most of us don't feel a great up-leveling. Real wages are stagnant and falling. Resource depletion and climate change are accelerating. Weapons of mass destruction—nuclear, biological, and technological—harbor in the shadows. Our existing institutions, rife with conflict and entropy, seem ill equipped to manage themselves—let alone a rapidly changing world. How do we reconcile the growing potential of humanity with the real risk that humanity won't make it at all?

The answer lies in doing what life does everywhere. The answer is *to scale*. The evidence I have for this comes from the natural world itself. Look closely and you'll see that nature isn't just sustainable; it is *scalable*. Give it an energy source and it'll keep growing and growing. It will fill in the evolutionary cracks and take advantage of every growth opportunity. Yet it doesn't accomplish this by limiting consumption and waste. It does this by creating full-circle ecosystems where nothing is wasted or lost. Everything is in service to everything else. And when the system gets too overgrown or sluggish, nature burns it up or washes it away and starts afresh. Evolution. Progress. Scale.

The same principle holds true in our human-made social, economic, and government systems. We're not going to save, conserve, or limit our way forward. That is scarcity thinking—and that never solved any problems. We must grow, build, and scale our way forward. We must be like nature and design, organize, and adapt our human-made systems so that they scale naturally, without waste or exploitation. It is only by creating a truly scalable world that we will unlock our collective potential, reshape our current systems to work better for all, and ultimately reach the stars and beyond.

This is where you come in. The entrepreneur. The business leader. The change agent. The hero. Yes, the hero. You see, the true role of the entrepreneur and business leader of our times has been miscast. It is not, as popular culture would have us believe, to start a company, exploit cheap labor, drive shareholder value, sell things off, and party like a rock star in an opulent but hollow mansion. This is an old, worn out "success" tape that plays in our collective consciousness and it needs to stop. This is not entrepreneurship. This is self-aggrandizing. If this is you, then god bless you but take your bling and shove it up your arse.

The true role of the 21st-century entrepreneur and business leader is among the noblest: to solve real problems in the world. And every true entrepreneur knows that the greater the problems, the greater the opportunities. The more efficiently, regeneratively, and creatively you can solve these problems, the more success and satisfaction you can attain and the greater the benefit to the whole. This is indeed the present-day hero's journey. And if we're going to solve the gargantuan-sized problems that beset planet earth, then we're going to need a lot of heroes.

We don't have to worry too much about those existing institutions that seem so stable, bureaucratic, and cancerous to the environment. Under pressure to scale, they will soon get burned up or washed away or they'll simply disintegrate under their own inertia. The way forward is by catalyzing a critical mass of systems-thinking entrepreneurs into the world—entrepreneurs who design and deliver innovative, problem-solving businesses, woven together by a passion for technology, ecology, and creating better ways of living and working. It is innovation that leads the way.

As Buckminster Fuller said, "We're all astronauts on spaceship earth." In that spirit, I encourage you to take the principles of Organizational Physics and get out there and solve problems on spaceship earth! That's the real purpose of your own and every business. Solve problems in the system. Do it efficiently, regeneratively, and creatively, and we will all prosper. Just remember, as you go about your journey, to keep a clear mind and a full heart . . . and don't fight the physics!

P.S. I'd love to hear from you. Visit me at www.OrganizationalPhysics.com and let me know about your journeys.

Appendix

About the Physics

The principles of Organizational Physics draw heavily on the laws of thermodynamics, evolution, and motion, as well as on systems theory. There are some differences and interpretations that, while not meaningful to the intent of this work, may warrant additional clarification.

Entropy in Open vs. Closed Systems

In physics and systems theory, there are two basic classifications of systems, closed and open. A closed system is one that can exchange energy (heat and work), but not matter, with its surroundings, while an "open" system exchanges matter and energy with its surroundings. In the 1800s, when the word "thermodynamics" was first coined, it was thought that the laws of thermodynamics only applied to closed or isolated systems.

We now know that no system is really closed or isolated (other than the summation of all systems that we call the universe or multiverse). This is because energy and matter are really the same thing and, with any attempt to define matter as a particle, we find that it resembles a wave or a new definition of matter such as quark–gluon plasma. Notice, too, that the more you try to define where one system begins and the other ends, the less you'll be able to identify a boundary. It's as if someone asked you to measure the coastline of California. How long is it? Well, the more closely you attempt to measure it, the longer it gets. Everything is an open system in interaction with everything else. Even a vacuum in space is teeming with energy and information and in open exchange with other systems.

As it turns out, how we apply the laws of thermodynamics (energy first flows to manage internal needs and only what's left can be used for integration) applies well to organizations of any size and is equally valid for all systems, closed and open. The founder of General Systems Theory, Bertrand von Bertalanffy, recognized that, according to the second law of thermodynamics, "the general trend of events in physical nature is towards states of maximum disorder and leveling down of differences, with the . . . heat death of the universe as the final outlook, when all energy is degraded into evenly distributed heat of low temperature, and the world process comes to a stop."[15] At the same time, Bertalanffy explains that

---

[15] Bertrand von Bertalanffy, *General Systems Theory* (New York: Braziller, 2003: 40-41).

...on the basis of the theory of open systems, the apparent contradiction between entropy and evolution disappears. In all irreversible processes, entropy must increase. Therefore, the change of entropy in closed systems is always positive; order is continually destroyed. In open systems, however, we have not only production of entropy due to irreversible processes, but also import of entropy which may well be negative. This is the case in the living organism which imports complex molecules high in free energy. Thus, living systems, maintaining themselves in a steady state, can avoid the increase of entropy, and may even develop towards states of increased order and organization" (*Ibid.*, p. 41)

What is "Energy?"

In classic physics, energy represents the ability to do work or to exert pulls or pushes on a physical object against the basic forces of nature like gravity and along a path of a certain length. In Organizational Physics, "energy" means any source of usable power. This includes not only the ability to exert a change on a physical object but also on an entire organization. It also includes energy equivalents such as money, resources, and clout. "Money" is really just a form of stored value or energy. It's used to make the exchange of products and services (other forms of stored energy) more efficient. "Resources" includes power sources that the organization has available to it, including the stored energy potential of the people, materials, natural resources, know-how, and capital equipment involved. "Clout" is the influence and good will that the organization has built up over time. From a business and personal perspective, if you think of energy as anything useful and desirable that can be made productive in the pursuit of success, you have a good working definition.

What is a "Force?"

In classic physics, "force" is a push or a pull on an object and is defined as either balanced or imbalanced. An imbalanced force is one in which either the push or the pull exert an unequal force and cause the object to move. If all forces are equal or balanced, there is no motion.

In Organizational Physics, a "force" is not a push or a pull on an object, but a force of change applied to an organization. The force in this case refers to the Producing, Stabilizing, Innovating, or Unifying forces, or some combination.

Just as in classic physics, one or more of the forces must be imbalanced in order to effect change. For example, if you want to drive the organization forward, you'll need to apply more Producing force and less of the others. To have the organization become more stable, you'll need more of the Stabilizing force. To help it discover new opportunities and avoid future threats, you'll need to amp up the Innovating force. To keep the organization unified as a whole, you'll need the Unifying force. Balancing and unbalancing the right forces, in the right sequence, while keeping entropy low and integration high—that's the art and science of Organizational Physics.

Index of Figures

CPSIA information can be obtained
at www.ICGtesting.com
Printed in the USA
LVOW11*0042270418
575091LV00004B/59/P